THE PURSUIT OF MARRIAGE ONENESS

The
PURSUIT
of MARRIAGE
ONENESS

The Key to Marital Success

DR. H. IRVING WILSON
XULON ELITE

Xulon Press Elite
2301 Lucien Way #415
Maitland, FL 32751
407.339.4217
www.xulonpress.com

Paperback ISBN-13: 978-1-6628-4699-1
Ebook ISBN-13: 978-1-6628-4700-4

Praise For
The Pursuit of Marriage Oneness

So many marriages within our churches are in dire need of reformation and restoration. The foundational scriptural principles that make a successful marriage have slowly eroded over generations. *The Pursuit of Marriage Oneness* insightfully details these precepts that can bring meaningful and lasting change to your marriage.

Steve Doan, D. Min. NAMA
Director of Grace and Peace Counseling Ministry

The Pursuit of Marriage Oneness is like no other marriage book I have read. Dr. Wilson brings his many years of experience in biblically-based marriage counseling and combines it with the wisdom that can only come from above. His focus on the oneness of the marriage union will encourage and guide those longing for a more intimate relationship with their spouse and God. This book will instruct and challenge you to experience the beauty of being one with your spouse in marriage.

Rabbi Matthew Salathe, D.Min.
Founder and President of Mosaic Ministries
A Primary Translator of the Tree of Life Bible

The Pursuit of Marriage Oneness has brilliantly developed and articulated the institution of marriage as a Godly design that is foundational to the health of the family and society. This work reflects years of marriage and family counseling experience and depth of scholarship. The institution of marriage has been misunderstood, misrepresented, and maligned over the years. Today marriage is trivialized, and hence the sacredness and permanence that are fundamental elements of its cohesiveness are missing. I gladly endorse this book. Readers will greatly benefit from its clarity and biblical depth.

Owen Facey, D.Min.
Senior Pastor, Genesis Christian Center
Professor, Author, and Seminar Speaker

I am so excited about *The Pursuit of Marriage Oneness*. It will challenge you to the profound meaning of the sacred institution of marriage. The thesis of the book is fresh and thought-provoking. Dr. Wilson has shown us the strength of marriage when God's principles are its intrinsic fabric. He guides us into strategic biblical precepts that will lead us on the path to enduring marital fulfillment. You will learn to navigate your marriage on course with tangible principles parabolically hidden in the scriptures. Congratulations to you, for you hold one of the best reads for building healthy marriages in your hands!

R. Pepe Ramnath, Ph.D. Environmental Microscopist, UN-NGO,
Senior Pastor of the Miramar Kingdom Community Center
Author and International Speaker

Dedication

This book is dedicated to the pioneering generations arising to take their place for reformation in rebuilding the ancient foundations of Judeo-Christian marriage: the Millennials, Generation Z, and the Silver Saints who answer the call to contend for them.

Contents

Part 1
Marriage Oneness:
The Pathway of Marital Fulfillment

Part 2
The Purity and Passion of Covenant Marriage:
The Pathway of Marital Intimacy

Part 3
Generative Oneness:
The Pathway of Marriage Longevity

Foreword
Sherron Wilson

Dear Reader,

$\mathcal{I}$ pray that this book will, in some way, be an answer to your prayer in having a more gratifying marriage. I believe you will find fresh manna in its pages. Most couples are desirous and determined to bring and find fulfillment in their marriage relationships. But many marriages are under attack due to a lack of knowledge. However, this can change when both husband and wife endeavor to live out their union in covenant relationship through Jesus Christ, reflecting His love for His bride the Church (1John 4:9). This book tells you how.

As a Pastor and Christian Counselor for over two decades, my husband has ministered to married couples in their pursuit of marital happiness. This book was birthed out of Irving's yearning to help couples experience fulfillment in their relationship. Counseling to him is not a job but a calling. God gives revelation for marital satisfaction to those who ask Him. He gives His strength and instruction manual to God-seekers to realize the abundant married life.

Whether you have been married for fifty days or fifty years plus and whatever your stage or the state of your marital relationship, I believe this book will advance your desire for greater marital satisfaction. Irving has searched the Word of God and compiled precise information to promote your quest for marital happiness. The principles and teachings included herein are practical and scripturally referenced. This work highlights God's biblical ideals for couples as they embark on the exciting, unexplored, challenging, yet most joyous of life's natural journey. Pursuing marriage Oneness leads to perfecting and becoming one in purpose that reflects the image of Christ's love as the bridegroom and the Church as His bride.

As you read this book, you'll discover that God's plan for marriage is multifaceted in its design; sacrifice, commitment, intimacy, structure, and spiritual dynamics, all culminating in revealing God's gift of married love. I pray that each new day compels you to chase the likeness of Christ with resolve so that it will reflect in married joy and happiness. This book shows you how. Irving and I have not yet perfected our faith in Oneness but press daily with the joy of the Lord towards "a more perfect union."

May your marital joy be full,

Sherron.

Preface

The Pursuit of Marriage Oneness

*T*his book aims to give a comprehensive exposition of the meaning of marriage oneness. It explores the path of the mystery of oneness. It offers the means to sustain the state of oneness for marriage success and its potential for generative transmission. This work is built on the foundation of God's infallible, efficacious, ancient, and contemporary Word.

All discussions are rooted in scriptural truths that are the cornerstone for a successful marriage. This content includes biblically-based marriage values, instruction, and concepts. The overall goal is to present the scriptural blueprint for a fulfilling marriage that glorifies God in theory and practice.

In 2007–2008, the Barna Group conducted studies on divorce rates in America. The research reported that Christians are just as likely to divorce as are non-Christians. The study further confirmed its findings through tracking studies conducted each year.

What is the problem when the world and the Church have a 50 percent divorce rate? Are some Christian marriages based on the world's philosophies or the Word? If it is the former, then we cannot expect different results from the world. The adage for the definition of "insanity": "Doing the same thing repeatedly and expecting different results" applies here. I have had couples that asked me why God has not blessed their marriage. In a brief discussion, the root cause is that they are subconsciously living according to the pattern of the world.

I have observed a misalignment between the biblical truths of marriage and the principles that many couples believe and practice in their daily lives. I submit that we have the same divorce rate as the world because we broadly adhere to the same foundational precepts and principles in conducting our marriages (Rom. 12:1–2).

The way to a rewarding marriage is in the manual produced by the One who invented marriage. God has guaranteed us that if we keep His Word on our lips and hearts and are "careful to do everything written in it," we will be prosperous and successful (Josh. 1:8). Rest assured that He is able and faithful to His covenant promises (Isa. 55:11). Therefore, we are confident; that when Abba Father declares and begins the work of oneness in a bride and bridegroom at the altar, He is faithful to perform for those who love him and keep his commandments (Phil. 1:6).

I discovered that so many married couples did not believe in the scriptural blueprint for marriage. It was not that they consciously rejected the biblical truths. It was not in their consciousness that they were living by a worldview of maladaptive thought patterns contrary to the Word of God. These patterns primarily derive from social learning, family traditions, entertainment media, and societal norms. Some couples were so immersed in the world's philosophy and living by its principles that they lived a lifestyle of ongoing competition and conflict. These Christians are sometimes confused about why they experience such seemingly unending frustration as born-again believers.

Christian marriages have slowly become an aberration from covenant marriage like the proverbial frog in boiling water. Christians have a renewed spirit, but our mind needs to be transformed by the Word and the Spirit of God to realize the mind of Christ (1 Cor. 2:16). Scriptural truths must replace false precepts, resulting in transformative behavioral change (Jn. 17:17). Christians must proactively return to the ancient foundations of Judeo-Christian values and traditions of marriage. The goal of oneness is a daily walk and not a final destination (Phil. 3:12). Marriage oneness is a journey with three; threefold cord with the bride, the groom, and Jesus, who is the way, the truth, and the life of the union. This book seeks to direct your hearts and steps on this journey of oneness into marriage fulfillment.

Acknowledgments

First, I would like to thank my clients for giving me the privilege and honor to walk with them to pursue marriage oneness toward a more perfect union. You have enriched this literary work, and you have enriched my marriage. Sherron and I thank you. I owe special gratitude to my sister, Norma Daniel, for her unwavering encouragement and support. I am grateful to my friend Dr. Percy Ricketts, a psychotherapist, who has cheered me on and offered helpful suggestions. Pastor Scott Ustick for his extraordinary encouragement and his great confidence in this work's potential to be a valuable contribution to the Christian community. Ruthven Mereigh has been a faithful prayer partner in offering up this work to the Lord. I thank Dr. Steve Doan, Pastoral Counselor, who has made insightful contributions to this work. Rabbi Matthew Salathe generously served as a Hebrew and Greek consultant unveiling scriptural insights in linguistic and cultural contexts. Above all, to God be the glory!

Part 1

Marriage Oneness:

The Pathway of Marital Fulfillment

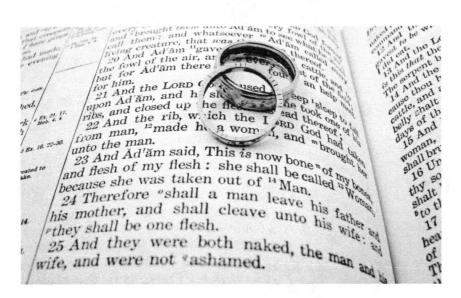

Chapter 1

Understanding Marriage Oneness
Unveiling the Mystery of the Marital Union

What Is Marital Oneness?

God performed the first wedding. The Lord described the joining of the first man and the first woman as united into one:

> Then the LORD God made a woman from the rib, and he brought her to the man. "At last!" the man exclaimed. "This one is bone from my bone, and flesh from my flesh!" She will be called woman, because she was taken from man. This explains why a man leaves his father and mother and is joined to his wife, and the two are united into one. (Gen.2:22–24)

Echad is the Hebrew word for "one" in this verse. Strongs defines *echad* as "a unified group." Adam and Eve became a unified couple at the marriage altar. What was God's ultimate purpose for this union? In the Book of Romans, the apostle Paul writes:

> Therefore I urge you, brothers and sisters, in view of God's mercy, to offer your bodies as a living sacrifice,

holy and pleasing to God—this is your true and proper worship. Do not be conformed to the pattern of this world, but be transformed by the renewing of your mind. Then you will be able to test and approve what God's will is-his good, pleasing and perfect will (Rom.12:1–2).

God wants all Christians to have his good, pleasing, and perfect will. But specifically, what is God's "good, pleasing, and perfect will" for marriage? God's good, pleasing, and perfect will for marriage is oneness. Belief in oneness is a couple's confidence and conviction that they are one (Heb.11:1). God supernaturally makes the bride and groom one. The practical aspect of oneness is the work of faith expressing itself through love (Jm. 2:17). The apostle Paul describes marital oneness as a great mystery that illustrates the union of Christ and the Church:

"A man leaves his father and mother and is joined to his wife, and the two are united into one. This is a great mystery, but it is an illustration of the way Christ and the Church are one" (Eph. 5:31–32, NLT).

Couples leave their fathers and mothers to become one at the marital altar. The matrimonial altar represents unity, commitment, and sacrificial love. God administers and creates one out of two. Subsequently, God commands that no man separate what he has joined together (Mk. 10:9). Thus, working out marriage oneness into practical reality is for a lifetime (Prov.4:18). Marital oneness is both a destination and a journey. It is a declaration of imputed oneness at the altar and a journey in the progressive walk of marital bonding.

Marriage oneness involves a couple merging their material and human resources to pursue their marital and family mission with a unified purpose. Spouses work as a team using biblical precepts and principles of marriage to serve each other and achieve their personal and common goals.

Premarital couples have often inquired how oneness will affect their identity. The analogy of the construction of a building can help bring clarity to this issue. When a building is under construction, there are many skilled workers. Generally, there are carpenters, plumbers, masons, electricians, and painters, to list a few. All work together to the desired end of completing the structure. They contribute their skills as a team, but they all maintain their distinct identity as to who they are. The same analogy applies to an orchestra producing a musical piece where each musician holds their unique place in the ensemble.

Similarly, couples with different marital roles and functions can work in synergy, utilizing their skills and gifting together in building their marriage and family. At other times spouses may pursue personal aspirations. Both situations can advance and enrich the marital union.

Marriage Oneness Is a Union of Three

Marriage oneness is a union of a husband and a wife with Jesus Christ as the head of that union. Creating oneness at the altar is the first impartation of God in covenant marriage. Such covenant unions adhere to the biblical values, instructions, and precepts that nurture and govern marriage. The first act of marriage is to receive God's declaration of oneness by faith. Married couples may not feel like one at the altar. However, God has made them one.

As we earlier stated, God instituted the first marriage when he brought Eve to Adam in the Garden of Eden and united them as one (Gen.2:18–25). Marriage is a calling. Adam did not initiate his marriage; it was God's call. It is a sacred ceremony that God continues to perform today. The first act of marriage is the spiritual induction into oneness. Couples receive the gift of each other by faith.

Marriage is inaugurated with spiritual and natural acts of oneness. The spiritual act occurs when a husband and a wife confess their vows and believe in their heart that "they are no longer two but one flesh" (Mark 10:8). The bride and groom become a new creation of one. This oneness is the spiritual consummation of the marriage administered from Heaven. The natural act of oneness declares the man and woman as husband and wife. The physical consummation of the marriage, the sexual act, seals the marriage union.

Holiness: Pathway to Marital Oneness

God desires marrieds to be holy. The pathway of marital oneness is to walk in holiness. God calls us to be holy, for he is holy (1 Pet. 1:16). The pursuit of God engenders holiness. Walking in holiness impels the pursuit of marital happiness; to love your spouse "just as Christ loved the Church and gave himself up for her" (Eph. 5:25). Authentic intimacy with God shapes your relationship with your spouse. Be in a continuous state of seeking righteousness, and marital joy will follow (Matt.6:33). Holiness is an attribute of God and the core of expressed oneness in marriage. God shares his holiness with us through the indwelling of His Holy Spirit that we may walk in Him (Heb. 12:10).

In an analogy between Christ and the Church, and husbands and wives, the apostle Paul states that Christ's sacrificial love makes the Church holy. The apostle also asserts that a husband's sacrificial love can facilitate his wife's holiness through his spiritual leadership. Paul explains that a husband's ministry of God's Word to his wife, primarily through his life, is a powerful Christian witness toward greater oneness:

> Husbands, love your wives, just as Christ loved the
> Church and gave himself up for her to make her holy,
> cleansing her by the washing with water through
> the Word, and to present her to himself as a radiant

Church, without stain or wrinkle or any other blemish, but holy and blameless. (Eph. 5:25–27)

In the same manner, a wife's virtuous conduct can lead her husband to spiritual transformation:

"In the same way, wives, be subject to your own husbands. Then, if some are disobedient to the Word, they will be won over without a word by the way you live" (1 Pet. 3:1, NETB).

Oneness: Pathway to Marital Joy

God desires marrieds to be happy. One of His commands to Israel demonstrates his desire for a husband and wife to pursue oneness at the inception of marriage. It also reveals how much God desires married couples to be happy. God instructs husbands to begin their honeymoon with the spirit of giving. He gave instructions that facilitate conditions for a husband's undistracted devotion in bringing happiness to his wife:

If a man has recently married, he must not be sent to war or have any other duty laid on him. For one year, he is to be free to stay at home and bring happiness to the wife he has married (Deut.24:5).

The implication is that a husband should have unbroken companionship for one year without extended travel away from his home. He should also not engage in any major community responsibilities during that time. That arrangement gave the married couple quantity and quality time for bonding and building physical, emotional, and spiritual intimacy. God places top priority from the inception of marriage on a husband to bring happiness to his wife. God underscores the need for married couples to intentionally reserve time together for personal, social, and spiritual engagements. The principal emphasis in God's instruction is giving, with the husband assuming the leadership role in modeling the love of Christ to His Bride, the Church.

God in the Proverbs counsels married couples to be faithful, be blessed, and enjoy each other (Prov.5:18). The Lord also dedicated the book of Song of Songs exclusively to celebrating marital love as one of His choicest gifts to humans. He desires that married couples find the joy and happiness of marriage in Him, "For everything comes from him, and exists by his power and is intended for his glory" (Rom.11:36).

Giving Is the Principal Virtue of Marriage Oneness

Giving is the principal virtue of oneness. The Lord God epitomizes love as giving. The Scripture declares that God so loved the world that he gave his only begotten Son (Jn. 3:16). Christ laid down his life for us as a sacrifice. There is no greater love (Jn. 15:13). It is such love that spouses give to each other by imitating Christ (Eph. 5:28–29, 1 Cor. 11:1). In a covenant marriage, "it is more blessed to give than to receive" (Acts 20:30). Spouses demonstrate this love when they value their partner's needs above their own (Phil. 2:3–4).

Marriage Is Made in Heaven

Pursuing oneness requires rejecting this world's culture on marriage for a biblical worldview. Marriage is a sacred institution. God is continuously registering marriage covenants where sincere men and women make sacred vows to each other. One cannot have an enduring and fulfilling marriage without God, for he is the author and administrator of this institution. Marriages are made in Heaven.

Matrimony is a holy sacrament. God holds the exclusive right to officiate at every wedding and give away the bride. The Lord joined together every legitimate married couple (Mk. 10:9). God is the spiritual Father who gave away the bride when He brought

Eve to Adam. God actually walked Eve "down the aisle" to Adam (Gen. 2:22).

If you are married, God was at your wedding to perform the mystery of oneness. If you are a wife, God was the spiritual Father who gave you away to your husband. If you are a husband, your "wife is from the Lord" (Prov. 19:14). If you plan to get married, your heavenly Father will be at your wedding to administer the oath of oneness and give away the bride. When you repeat your vows, he unites you as one. The officiating clergy certifies the heavenly mystery with the declaration of, "I now pronounce you husband and wife."

Oneness on Earth as it Is in Heaven

The first act of marriage is God's impartation of the mystery of oneness. Oneness is a heavenly concept. God desires that the principle of oneness be "done on earth as it is in Heaven" (Matt. 6:10). In Heaven, the Godhead of the Father, the Son, and the Holy Spirit are one (Deut. 6:4). Jesus asserted, "I and the Father are One" (Jn. 10:30). The Lord God is also one with the saints (Jn. 14:20, 1 Cor. 6:17). Jesus's final prayer on earth is that the Church unite as one (Jn. 17:22–23).

The Meaning of Marriage

The Law of First Mention is a theological principle used to study the Bible. Essentially, it says that the first time an idea, principle, precept, or doctrine appears in the Bible establishes its foundational meaning. Based on the original passage, all subsequent scriptures on marriage are interpreted and more fully developed. Marriage is first mentioned in Genesis:

"Therefore, shall a man leave his father and his mother, and shall cleave unto his wife, and they shall be one flesh" (Gen. 2:24, KJV).

The final intent in this verse is to become "one flesh." Leaving father and mother and cleaving to each other engender oneness. The concept of oneness is developed subsequently in the Scriptures (Mk. 19:5, Mk. 10:8, Eph. 5:22–33). The ultimate goal for holy matrimony is to glorify God. The manifestation of God's glory in marriage is oneness. Conclusively, the first mention of marriage is that spouses are one. According to the Law of First Mention, marital oneness would be the fundamental meaning of marriage. All subsequent scripture on marriage contributes to advancing the understanding of marital oneness. We will now discuss the required prerequisites to enter the path of the practical aspect of oneness.

Leaving to Become One

Leaving father and mother is the first act in the prescriptive process for a successful marriage. Leaving is a wholehearted commitment by a married couple to create a new home and family. It brings finality to a husband and wife regarding their role in their parental household.

Leaving entails establishing a different family institution (Eph. 5:31–32). A husband and wife must leave their former abode's physical, social, and psychological structures and create a family institution unique for every couple. It is a new institution created by a husband and wife who would share their lives for a lifetime.

New responsibilities transition from the parental organization into couples establishing a home and family. However, adult children must love and honor their parents. Adult children should meet the needs of their parents where circumstances demand. They must repay parents and grandparents to be pleasing to God (1 Tim. 5:4).

Cleaving to Become One

The second prerequisite to practical oneness is cleaving to your spouse (Gen. 2:24). The Hebrew word for cleave is *dabaq*. The English Standard Version translates it as "hold fast." The Christian Standard Bible translates it as "bond." Cleaving is a bonding experience. Bonding is getting to know your spouse. "To know" in Hebrew thought is to have a personal and intimate relationship. The Book of Genesis states that "Adam knew his wife" (Gen. 4:1). Although this verse refers to sexual relations, it also implies an intimate social and emotional relationship.

Jehovah God, speaking to Abraham, declared, "Now I know that you fear God" (Gen. 22:12). This statement does not mean that the Lord did not know Abraham feared God. The word *yada* (know) used here implies that God had personal interactional experiences with Abraham. A similar verse expresses God's relationship with Moses:

"He made known his ways to Moses, his deeds to the people of Israel" (Ps. 103:7).

The Israelites saw the miracles of God. Moses had personal encounters with God (Ps. 103:7). The Lord spoke "to Moses face to face as one speaks to a friend" (Ex. 33:11). This intimacy implies what cleaving means. It is an authentic, vulnerable, and intimate face-to-face interaction between a husband and his wife.

Cleaving to God

Cleaving to God is the foundational relationship to achieve oneness. It is cleaving to God that we are enabled to cleave to our spouse to foster intimacy (Jn. 23:8). Cleaving is reciprocal. God invites us to draw near him, and he will draw near us (Jm. 4:8). God not only gives the invitation but initiates the process when he extends both arms to us on Calvary. Our bond with God is through his Word and the Spirit. Obedience to God's Word binds us to him, for He is the Word (Jn. 1:1). We must first be intimately attached to Jesus to bear the fruit of oneness. Jesus said:

"I am the vine; you are the branches. If you remain in me and I in you, you will bear much fruit; apart from me, you can do nothing" (Jn. 15: 5).

Pursuing marriage oneness is first pursuing oneness with God (1 Cor. 6:17). The fruit of oneness is the fruit of marital love. Only through cleaving to Jesus, the Vine, can we succeed in marriage. As Christians, we possess the very nature of God, for we are partakers of his spirit (2 Pet. 1:3–4). God's nature empowers us to work out the mystery of the sacred union (Col. 1:27). This new creation of oneness is achieved most successfully in couples who first cleave unto the Lord to work out the mystery of their union (Phil. 2:12).

Unveiling the Mystery of Marital Oneness

In the Book of Ephesians, the apostle Paul compares marriage to the union between Christ and the Church. In this epistle, Paul describes the concept of "one flesh" in marriage as a mystery:

"For this reason, a man will leave his mother and his father and be united to his wife, and the two will become one flesh. This is a profound mystery, but I am talking about Christ and the Church" (Eph. 5:31–32).

The word "mystery" comes from the Greek *mysterion*, defined as "that which awaits disclosure or interpretation, and revealed only to the initiated." This meaning is similar to the practices of some fraternal organizations today. Such organizations have secrets that only members can know. A person must join the organization to learn and experience its secrets.

Paul was alluding to how couples enter marital oneness. Married couples must believe and live out biblical values and principles of marriage to know its secrets and experience its fruit. This fruit manifests in physical, emotional, social, and spiritual harmony in a couple's relationship. Married partners can live a lifetime and not enter into the secrets of the mystery of marital oneness. They can fail to believe in and live by the principles of marriage oneness.

Oneness Revealed through Faith

Faith is the substance of oneness. There is no natural way to achieve oneness. It is impossible without faith. God promised Abraham that he and Sarah would have a child in their old age, which was impossible in the natural. The promise manifested because Abraham "was strengthened in his faith and gave glory to God" (Rom. 4:19–20).

God declares that the righteous shall live by faith (Gal. 3:11). This truth also applies to living your marriage. The strength to achieve marital success is the joy in believing that God can sustain your oneness (Ps. 73:26). The faith of oneness is the belief in the mystery of the marriage union. Faith is what makes marriage potent. Couples reflect God's glory in oneness (2 Cor. 3:18). This transformation in marriage is the work of faith. When a married couple believes in God's declaration about their union, their faith is counted as oneness (Rom. 4:3).

Faith in oneness is faith in the Word of God. Faith in the Word of God is faith in God (Jn. 1:1, Rom. 10:17). The belief in oneness is based not on what you see or feel about your relationship. The faith of oneness is believing in what God said about you two becoming one (Matt. 19:6).

Oneness Revealed through Obedience

Jesus explains that only those who believe and walk in righteousness can enter into the secrets of the kingdom. Jesus frequently spoke to the multitudes in parables. The disciples asked him why he spoke to the crowds in parables. Jesus answered:

13

"The secret of the Kingdom of God has been given to you. But to those on the outside, everything is said in parables" (Mk. 4:11).

Jesus was explaining that only those who are true disciples are privy to the secrets of the kingdom. The disciples believed in and followed Jesus. Only those who submit to God receive the revelation of the mysteries. The Word of God informs us that the Lord makes his secrets known only to those who obey him (Ps. 25:14). God reveals the secret of oneness and thus marital fulfillment to those who have faith in their union and walk in obedience to the scriptural precepts of covenant marriage.

Married couples must enter into oneness by faith and subsequently, through obedience to the biblical precepts of marriage, to experience the blessings of marriage (Ps. 133:1–3). Marital oneness, at its core, is the outworking of the love of God in your heart to your spouse (Rom. 5:5). A couple's intimacy with each other is positively related to their intimacy with Jesus Christ. As couples become more submitted to the love of Christ, they become more intimate with their spouse (2 Cor. 3:18).

But how do married couples enter into the mystery of the functional experience of oneness? We will explore the state of the marital union in Chapter 2 by discussing the two aspects of marital oneness, namely positional oneness, and practical oneness.

Chapter 2

The State of the Marital Union
Positional Oneness and Practical Oneness

*M*arriage begins with God's declaration that a man and a woman have become one (Mk. 10:8). This union is the mystery of oneness. The bride and bridegroom spiritually consummate their marriage by faith. This consummation occurs when they confess their vows and the officiating minister confirms their status as husband and wife. The Christian life stands on faith. Faith is the foundation of marriage success. God rewards the Christian through faith. Marriage fulfillment is the reward of faith expressing itself through love:

"And without faith, it is impossible to please God because anyone who comes to him must believe that he exists and that he rewards those who earnestly seek him" (Matt. 11:6).

This belief in oneness is the first act of marriage for a man and woman. It is an act of faith, from singleness to oneness. Marital love is released through faith when a couple agrees with God that "they are no longer two but one flesh" (Matt. 19:6). God sets the relationship sequence for marriage. The spiritual union precedes the physical consummation of sexual unity. Let us now examine the two phases of marital oneness: positional and practical oneness.

Positional Righteousness: Made Righteous

Using an apperceptive approach by understanding the concept of righteousness can better inform our comprehension of marriage oneness. Righteousness is God's gift by grace through faith. Positional righteousness and practical righteousness are the two stages of holy consecration. We begin with positional righteousness.

Positional righteousness is God's work of grace through faith. We receive this gift on being declared righteous on repentance of sin and confession of faith in our Lord Christ Jesus (Rom. 5:1). In the courts of Heaven, we are legally declared righteous. This standing is our new legal position. It is our spiritual identity in Christ. We become a part of the family of God. The following scripture affirms this imputed righteousness:

"**We have been made holy** through the sacrifice of the body of Jesus Christ once and for all... He has made perfect forever by one sacrifice, those who are being made holy" (Heb. 10:10,14, emphasis added).

Here our position in Christ is perfect righteousness. This "righteousness is given through faith in Jesus Christ to all who believe, apart from any works of the Law" (Rom. 3:22–24). Our faith is credited as righteousness (Rom. 4:5). However, our declared righteous position is not yet fully reflected in our daily living in the natural realm. We must work out our legal position through the Holy Spirit to become a practical reality throughout our lifetime.

Practical Righteousness: Being Made Righteous

Practical righteousness is God's continued work of grace through faith. God gives the desire and power to walk in the truth. Works verify belief, for faith by itself is dead (Jm. 2:17). Our work certifies our faith and is the evidence of our faith in our pursuit of righteousness (1 Tim. 6:11). Practical righteousness is the lifelong process of being made holy:

- By one sacrifice, he has made perfect forever those who **are being made holy** (Heb. 10:14, emphasis added).

- May God himself, the God of peace, sanctify you through and through. May your whole spirit, soul, and body be kept blameless at the coming of the Lord Jesus Christ. The one who calls you is faithful, and he will do it (1 Thess. 5:23–24).

- Therefore, my dear friends, as you have always obeyed—not only in my presence but now much more in my absence—continue to work out your salvation with fear and trembling, for it is God who works in you to will and to act in order to fulfill his good purpose (Phil. 2:12–13, emphasis added).

Positional Oneness: Made One

Now, let us discuss marital oneness applying the concepts of righteousness. Positional oneness is God's gift of grace through faith. It is a belief in your marital identity of being one. As previously stated, the principles of positional righteousness can inform our understanding of positional oneness in marriage. Positional oneness is a spiritual declaration from the courts of Heaven that earthly courts subsequently legalize. God's spiritual pronouncement at weddings is that the bride and the groom are "no longer two but one flesh" (Mk. 10:8). It is a spiritual act that is not apparent to the natural human senses and the mind. It is a state imparted by God and received in faith by the bride and groom on the confession of their marriage vows.

Positional oneness is the truth that a married couple becomes one instantaneously. A couple's identity as husband and wife is that they are spiritually one. The married couple receives this declared state by faith, pledging "till death do us part." Positional oneness is your marital identity, emanating from your primary identity in Christ Jesus. This identity of oneness is who you are, a unified pair, regardless of the situation or circumstances occurring in your marriage that seems to indicate otherwise. Marital problems do not change the fact of your oneness.

We can draw general principles for understanding positional oneness using our understanding of positional righteousness. The married couple is declared one at the altar without any action on their part. The bride and groom have not engaged in any bonding activity as husband and wife to engender oneness. They are one by the heavenly proclamation on agreeing to become husband and wife. When a couple declares with their mouth and believes in their heart the truth of their marital vows, God credits their faith as oneness.

The spiritual position of a married couple is perfect oneness. God creates marriage oneness. As is the legal status of righteousness, the legal status of oneness is not yet fully manifested in the natural realm. The evidence that couples are one is the assurance and conviction that they are one (Heb. 11:1). They believe that God faithfully performs his Word (Rom. 4:21).

Faith Is the First Work of Marriage Oneness

Faith is the first work of marriage. The essence of the marriage vow is a declaration of commitment, sacrifice, and the pledge of faith. The traditional Protestant vow reads:

> I (small line here), take you, (small line here), to be
> my wedded husband/wife, to have and to hold, from
> this day forward, for better, for worse, for poorer, in
> sickness and in health, to love and to cherish, till

death do us part, according to God's holy ordinance,
and to that, I pledge you my faith.

The pledge of faith is the spiritual and initial consummation of the marriage. This act of faith is the first act of the couple. Married couples spiritually become one. God imparts oneness, and the officiating minister presents the couple as husband and wife. It is noteworthy that a violation of one's vows is defined as "broken faith" (Mal. 2:14, CJB).

Realizing our oneness at the altar is the first work of faith to pursue marital oneness. The first act of our salvation experience is to believe the Word of God. Jesus declared that "the work of God is to believe in the one he has sent" (Jn. 6:29). Similarly, the first work of marriage is that the married couples believe in God's Word, that they are one (Eph. 5:31).

A Paradigm Shift from Singleness to Oneness

Married couples experience a paradigm shift from singleness to oneness. Belief in this spiritual truth of oneness is the foundation for a successful marriage. God's Word declares that your belief system "determines the course of your life" (Prov. 4:23, NLT). Believing that you are one will determine the course of your married life. You will be motivated to act like one. Acting as one means spouses love each other like loving themselves (Eph. 5:28–29).

A husband and wife who pursue oneness would experience a paradigm shift in thinking and behavior as they align themselves with the marital precepts in God's Word. Therefore, faith in oneness is the initial prerequisite for a couple to transform from the psychological perspective of singleness to oneness.

Practical Oneness: Being Made One

The fruit of oneness is not automatic. It will manifest through faith, love, and perseverance (Phil. 2:12). Practical oneness is God's continued work of grace through faith in living out your marriage identity as one. Practical oneness reflects how a married couple walks in unity with the scriptural precepts governing and nurturing the marriage union (Eph. 5:21–23). Practical oneness is working out your imputed oneness (Phil. 2:12).

Let us use the game of soccer to clarify the concept of practical oneness. We will select the position of center-forward for our analogy. The player must work out the practical reality of the position to various degrees by essentially following the rules and strategies of the position of center forward. The player must also further define success as a center-forward by scoring goals in collaborating with her teammates. Similarly, couples must work out the reality of their declared position of oneness at the altar in daily actions that reflect faith in God and love for their spouse.

Belief in oneness precedes walking in oneness (Matt. 21:22). Faith in oneness by itself is dead (Jm. 2:17). Faith must show evidence by deeds of love to your spouse. In practical oneness, married couples are being made one and must work out their oneness as a labor of love. This labor of love demonstrates "love, joy, peace, forbearance, goodness, kindness, faithfulness, gentleness and self-control" (Gal. 5:22–23).

The true faith of oneness involves an intellectual assent and a belief from the heart, which possesses an emotional component. The Bible explains that authentic faith is of the mind and the heart (Rom.10:9–10). It is such faith that leads to the actions that reflect practical oneness. Genuine belief generates action. The couple who believes they are one will reflect that conviction in love for God and spouse.

Practical Oneness Is Progressive

Practical Oneness is progressive. The love between a husband and a wife increases as they release the love of God from their heart. The apostle Paul assures us that practical oneness is a process:

"May the Lord make your love increase and overflow for each other and for everyone else, just as ours does for you" (1 Thess. 3:12).

A couple being one is an accomplished truth in the spiritual realm. However, progress is provisional in the natural sphere. It is contingent, based on submission to God. The following passage exemplifies this concept where God admonishes Israel:

> If my people who are called by my name will humble themselves and pray and seek my face and turn from their wicked ways, then I will hear from Heaven, and I will forgive their sins and heal their land. (2 Chron. 7:14, emphasis added)

God's restoration of Israel was conditioned on the people's repentance as chronicled by Solomon. Similarly, God declares married couples as one. Subsequently, marital success is predicated upon couples walking in the principles governing and nurturing the marriage union.

God has promised that our faith in oneness will result in experiences of marital fulfillment if we persevere and faint not (Gal. 6:9). Couples progressively manifest maturity by living the marital truths of the Word of God. When spouses submit to God, He is faithful to carry on to completion the work he began at the marriage altar (Phil. 1:6).

Faith of Marital Oneness Activates Love

Mature faith is living what you believe (Jm. 2:22). Living out your belief in oneness is caring for your spouse daily as you do for yourself (Eph. 5:28). The faith of oneness is "activated and expressed through love" (Gal. 5:6 Amp). Therefore, the married couple's ever-increasing faith in their union produces ever-increasing love and intimacy in their marriage.

As we previously cited, people live their lives according to what they believe in their hearts (Prov. 23:7). The apostle Paul asserted that faith "makes you love others" (Gal. 5:6, CEV). The belief in oneness (that you and your spouse are one) impels husbands to love their wives as their own bodies. Paul affirms that "he who loves his wife loves himself" and should care for her "just as Christ does the Church" (Eph. 5:28–29).

The faith of oneness drives marital relationships. When a husband believes that he is one with his wife, he identifies with her needs and desires as his very own. When a wife accepts that she is one with her husband, she regards his needs and desires as her very own. This conviction and devotion testify to faith expressing itself through love (Gal. 2:20).

Perfecting the Faith of Marital Oneness

God initiates the faith in oneness that births love in marriage at the altar. God promised that on our obedience, he would bless the marital union. God is faithful to bring the oneness recorded in Heaven to become a practical reality on earth (Phil. 1:6). Our love grows through Jesus, the "pioneer and perfector of faith" (Heb. 12:2).

When we submit to living by kingdom principles in our marriage, we bear the fruit of the Spirit. The life of the Spirit is progressively evident in the joy of marital love. In the pursuit of oneness, couples are fulfilling their unique work of marriage, which God prepared in advance for them to do (Eph. 2:10).

In salvation, we show our faith through our works. We do not pursue righteousness to be saved. Our pursuit of holiness demonstrates that we are saved. Similarly, exhibiting the virtues of oneness is not to become one. God already declared at the altar that married couples are one. Working out oneness is faith in action, expressing love to your spouse, bearing the evidence of your oneness (Phil. 2:12). The apostle James asserts this concept. The following passage exemplifies the relationship between faith and works of love:

"Show me your faith without your works (love), and I will show you my faith by my works(love)... Faith and actions (love) work together so that faith is made complete" (Jm. 2:18, 22, parentheses added).

Marriage Oneness Begins in Faith and Continues by Faith

In the Book of Galatians; the apostle Paul admonished the Galatian Church regarding faith and works of the Law:

> You foolish Galatians! Who has cast an evil spell on you? For the meaning of Jesus Christ's death was made clear to you as if you had seen a picture of his death on the cross. Let me ask you this one question: Did you receive the Spirit by obeying the Law of Moses? Of course not! You received the Spirit because you believed the message you heard about Christ. How foolish can you be? After starting your new lives in the Spirit, why are you now trying to become perfect by your own human effort? (Gal. 3:1–3 NLT).

The Galatians had come to believe that additional works of righteousness were necessary for their salvation. They were also trusting in themselves to live a victorious Christian life, apart from faith in the indwelling of the Holy Spirit. They trusted in their own works instead of faith in Christ's finished work on the cross.

The apostle Paul admonished the Church in Galatia. He challenged them to explain why they began their salvation experience by the Spirit and then began living by human effort. The Galatians entered the kingdom of God by faith in Christ through the Spirit. The work of salvation "is accomplished from start to finish by faith" (Rom. 1:17, NLT). In the same way, married life is by faith in God's truth of oneness from start to finish. Oneness begins in faith at the altar and continues in faith for a lifetime.

Marriage Oneness by the Pattern of the Word

I have observed that many couples follow the path of beginning their marriage by faith in the truth of their spiritual oneness and later begin striving to live out their marriage through human effort. They recognize and agree that their marriage started with a spiritual act of God. But in our discussion, it becomes evident that they lived by generational family ideas and world philosophies. In most cases, they were unaware that they lived by the world's cultural norms. They were not living by faith in God's nuptial work of oneness.

These couples subconsciously conformed to societal norms. They live solely in the realm of the natural. The enemy of our soul has gradually lured Christians away from biblical truths, such that sacred marital precepts seem archaic. The Church needs a bold reformation, without apology, back to the foundational principles of married oneness. There is an urgent need for Christian couples to be sanctified, set apart from the world's culture regarding marriage. The Spirit is calling couples to be "renewed in knowledge" by the enduring Word of the Lord (Col. 3:10, Deut. 6:4). Godly marriages follow the pattern of the Word and not the pattern of the world. Successful marriages begin in the Spirit by faith and continue by faith in the One who is the author and perfector of the faith of marriage.

The Divine Faith of Marriage Oneness

Analogous to salvation, marriage begins in the Spirit by faith and must continue by faith to be successful. What we perceive of our condition in oneness in the natural should not deter our faith. What is essential is to be established in God's Word that two have become one. It is incongruous to begin by the Spirit and then alternate by living by what we perceive in the natural. Your spouse not acting like one does not negate God's Word that you are one. As Christians, we "live by faith, not by sight" (2 Cor. 5:7). As married couples, we love by faith and not by sight.

Spouses progressively express the manifestation of oneness in loving each other. This love is Christ living through Christian couples to realize their oneness (1 Jn. 2:20). The love spouses share is powered by faith (Gal. 5:6). Therefore, "let us keep our eyes fixed on Jesus, on whom our faith depends from beginning to end" (Heb. 12:2).

The Divine Rest of Marriage Oneness

The divine rest of oneness displays marital peace and harmony in marriages. Many Christians enter into marriage with the world's philosophy of contract partnership and not in covenant. They fail to enter by faith in the mystery of oneness. Subsequently, they do not act like one because they do not believe they are one. There are lots of bargaining, personal victories, competing visions, and independence. Couples that assimilate the world's culture on marriage do not build on the foundational precepts of marital oneness.

As previously stated, we acquire our imputed righteousness by faith. God's plan for Christians is that we live all aspects of our lives "by faith from first to last" (Rom. 1:17). The Israelites who left Egypt could not enter God's rest due to their lack of faith (Heb. 3:18–19). They had the good news preached to them, "but the message they heard was of no value to them because they did not share the faith of those who obeyed" (Rom. 4:2–3). Belief produces action.

The Israelites did not enter God's divine rest because they did not have faith in the message they heard and subsequently did not obey. Similarly, married couples must believe in the spiritual act of married oneness. Consequently, they will act on their belief, walking in God's marital truths, and enter the divine rest of marital harmony.

Manifest Oneness

Couples must agree with God on his declaration of the truth that they are one. There is power in accord with God (Matt. 18:19). Spouses' assurance is that their faith will progressively manifest into love in their marital journey (Gal. 5:6).

Oneness is activated when couples say their vows with faith. Spouses who believe what the Lord says they are progressively become what the Lord says they are (Mk. 10:8). The fruit of oneness faith would subsequently be evident in practical manifestations of married love.

Married couples demonstrate unity and love in their marriage when they have faith in their declared oneness. They manifest the evidence of that faith in the practical acts of love, for love expresses itself through faith. Married couples must affirm the truth of their oneness in living the biblical precepts and principles of marriage (Heb. 11:1).

Walking in the marital truths of God's Word translates into behaviors that increasingly reflect the love between Christ and the

Church (Eph. 5:21–33). As couples express their faith through love, they decreasingly narrow the gap between their perfect position of oneness and their functional state of being made one (Prov. 4:18).

Oneness is Your Marital Identity

Married couples glorify God when they walk in their marital identity of oneness. Couples find a refreshing harmony in the marriage relationship when they reject conformity to the world's values and philosophies and replace them with the sanctifying Word of Truth (Rom. 12:1–3). It is a shift from the world's culture to the culture of the Word.

Paul's counsel of beginning by faith in the Spirit and continuing by the same faith is the fundamental truth of marital success. It is impossible to please God without faith (Heb. 11:6). It is also impossible to please your spouse without confidence in your oneness. Couples should continue to live by faith in the generative principles of God's precepts on marriage. Trust in the Word of God on marriage leads to walking out the truth of oneness. Spouses are being transformed into the likeness of Christ into their marital identity of oneness (2 Cor. 3:18). Recognition of this developing identity increases spousal bonding, relational harmony, and intimacy.

Practical oneness is an ever-increasing marriage bonding that continues in spiritual, social, and emotional growth for a lifetime (2 Cor. 3:18, Phil. 2:12). In the pursuit of marital oneness, you are always on the journey to attain another goal. It is, however, not without a challenge, in unveiling the mystery of the consummate oneness. Married couples should press on with contentment toward what Jesus declared them to be: no longer two but one.

Chapter 3

Covenant Marriage
Mutual Belonging, Sacrifice, and Commitment

What is a Covenant?

*B*efore we embark upon our discourse on the marriage covenant, it would be helpful to clarify what is a covenant is from the Word of God. A covenant is a binding agreement between two persons or groups. It is a sacred accord meant to last a lifetime and may even apply to future generations.

Understanding covenant rituals in the Bible is an excellent place to begin our discussion, for the ritual acts are the symbolic meaning of covenant. There are several components in the execution of a covenant ritual. However, our discussion will focus on the two aspects that symbolize commitment and sacrifice, most applicable to the marriage covenant.

Let us examine the covenant ritual in the Scriptures between David and Jonathan. This covenant ritual involved the exchange of personal effects. David and Jonathan exchanged their robe, tunic, sword, bow, and belt (1 Sam. 18:3-4).

Clothes in the Bible represent the person. When the father in the parable of the prodigal son restored his son's identity within the family, he put the best robe upon him. The sword, bow, and belt represent the strength and resources that covenant partners commit to each other. Overall, the symbolisms amount to the commitment of the lives and resources of covenant partners to each other. They pledge to protect one another and be there for each other when needed, for a lifetime.

A significant aspect of the covenant ritual is sacrifice. An animal is killed to "cut" the covenant. God made such a covenant with Abraham (Gen.15). This facet of the covenant ritual symbolizes the dying to self of both partners to begin a new relationship to protect and support each other in all areas of life. Thus, the core of covenant is sacrifice and commitment.

The covenant God made with humanity personifies sacrifice and commitment. Jesus gave himself up for us. Christ took away our filthy clothing, symbolized by sin, and exchanged it for His robe of righteousness, which signifies justification from sin (Isa.64:6 & 61:10). Then He committed to be with us always even to the end of the age (Matt.28:20). Salvation is the ultimate expression of covenant. Jesus, who knew no sin, took our sins that we might become the righteousness of God (2 Cor. 5:21).

Marriage is a Covenant of Three

Marriage is a covenant (Jer. 31:32, Mal. 2:14, Prov. 2:17). The Judeo-Christian marriage is a covenant of three. The concept of a marriage covenant is unlike a social or business contract. God initiates the marriage covenant. He performs the mystery of marital oneness. Couples commit themselves in covenant with God and each other in a binding, inviolable, intimate relationship of unconditional love for a lifetime (Mk. 10:9).

The marriage covenant comprises vertical and horizontal facets. The vertical aspect is the couple agreeing with God that they are no longer two but one and submitting to Jesus Christ as head of the marriage union (Mk. 10:8). The horizontal interaction is the couple's committing themselves to each other for a lifetime (1 Sam. 18).

The marriage covenant entails an exchange of self with a pledge of love, friendship, and loyalty until death. Most importantly, God is at the center of the union to guide the bride and groom into marital fulfillment. God is faithful in keeping His covenant of love to those who love him and keep his commandments (Deut. 7:9). Those who walk in the scriptural precepts of marriage are assured that God is faithful to keep His covenant (Isa. 55:11). The marriage covenant is the essence of oneness. God imparts his blessings on marital unity (Ps. 133:1–3). The fundamental truth is that married couples are in union with God and each other, in a covenant of three.

The marriage covenant is recorded in Heaven and on earth. God writes the marriage covenant on the bride and groom's hearts with the conviction that they are one (Jer. 31:33, 1 Jn. 5:7). The bride and the groom record their covenant through their vows in giving themselves to each other and signing their marriage license.

Covenant Made by Sacrifice

Sacrifice establishes a covenant. God declares to his people Israel: "Bring my faithful people to me—those who made a covenant with me by giving sacrifice" (Ps. 50:5).

Covenant is made through sacrifice. The patriarchs Abraham, Isaac, and Jacob all made covenants with God by sacrifice (Gen.15, 26, 31). Sacrifices were offerings made unto the Lord. The nation of Israel offered sacrifices for a variety of situations. The principal purpose was to receive salvation and initiate, maintain, and restore a good relationship with God. The covenant sacrifice was something of great personal value without any defects. The Israelites offered sacrifices on the brazen altar. Similarly, the marriage covenant is the exchange of self as the sacrifice at the marriage altar.

Covenant Sacrifice is to Draw Near

The Hebrew word for sacrifice is *korban*. The Semitic root meaning of *korban* is "to draw close." The Israelites, therefore, offered up sacrificial offerings to draw near to God. Sin and trespass separated Israel from God. Sacrifices restored life and fellowship (Lev. 5, 6).

These sacrifices were a shadow of good things to come and not the reality themselves (Heb. 10:1). When the Messiah came, his blood washed away sins once and for all. The Holy Spirit now dwelt in the heart of man, drawing them unto himself by sacrifice (Heb. 10:10). The apostle Paul wrote:

"But now in Christ Jesus, you who were far away have been brought near by the blood of Christ" (Eph. 2:13).

Similarly, the bride and groom's gift of self at the altar is *korban*. They desire to draw near to each other by self-sacrifice. Sacrifice involves giving up something of value. The most significant value is self. Jesus asserted that there is no greater love than a person sacrificing their life for their friend (Jn. 15:13). Covenant spouses lay down their life for each other as a living sacrifice, holy and pleasing to God (Rom. 12:1–2). They are not their own. They have committed themselves to serving each other unconditionally, honoring each other above themselves.

Marriage Covenant is Commitment

The marriage offering of self initiates the journey of commitment and intimacy between a husband and a wife. The sacrifice takes place at the altar, the place of commitment. This sacrifice is an invaluable gift exchange. It is the total surrender of two wills to serve God and each other from the heart. A typical marriage vow expresses giving, belonging, self-sacrifice, and commitment:

I, (small line here), take you, (small line here), to be my wedded husband/wife, to have and to hold, from this day forward, for better, for worse, for richer, for poorer, in sickness and in health, to love and to cherish, till death do us part, according to God's holy ordinance, and to it, I pledge myself to you.

Some other wedding vows, such as the typical messianic version, emphasize covenant, as follows:

I, (small line here), take thee, (small line here), to be my wedded husband/wife. And I do promise and covenant, before God and these witnesses, to be thy loving and faithful wife/husband, in plenty and in want, in joy and in sorrow, in sickness and in health, as long as we both shall live.

A Covenant Takes Effect on Death

A covenant or testament takes effect upon death. The apostle Paul writes:

> For where there is a covenant, there must be the death of the one who made it. For a covenant is valid only when people are dead, for it is never in force when the one who made it lives (Heb. 9:16–17, NASB).

The validity of a covenant comes at the death of the one who made it. Marriage is a covenant. Therefore, a husband and a wife must "die" for the covenant to become effectual. The death required is being a living sacrifice. Spouses submit their lives in humility in service to God and each other. The submission of self epitomizes Paul's counsel to "submit to one another out of reverence for Christ" (Eph. 5:21). It is death by sacrifice explained by the apostle Paul:

> For Christ's love compels us because we are convinced that one died for all, and therefore all died.

And he died for all, that those who live should no
longer live for themselves but for him who died for
them and was raised again. (2 Cor.5:14–15).

Marriage covenant requires us to no longer live for ourselves.
We are not our own. We die to ourselves and begin a new walk with
our covenant partner. When we experience conflict and unhap-
piness in our relationships, covenant partners endure and work
through their issues with confidence in their oneness and faith
in God (Rom. 5:5). Dying to self is not self-seeking (1 Cor.13:5).
When your spouse hurts you, you die to yourself when you respond
with forgiveness and caring for their emotional healing. We imitate
Christ in loving our spouse as Christ loves the Church and gave his
life for her. Spouses die to themselves with honor, giving preference
to each other in all things (Rom. 12:10). The marriage covenant
manifests when couples die to themselves. The marriage covenant
is effectual when spouses die daily to self, ensuing into the fruit of
marital joy and happiness.

Living Sacrifice to Abundant Love

Our Lord Jesus illustrated the principle of death that brings life:
"Verily, verily I tell you, unless a kernel of wheat falls to the
ground and dies, it remains only a single seed. But if it dies it produces many seeds" (Jn. 12:24).

Couples must die by sacrifice to transition from a "single seed"
into the abundant harvest of oneness. Paul counsels spouses to live
a life of "dying," exemplified by spouses loving each other as they
love their own bodies (Eph. 5:28).

It is sacrificial death that births unity and marital harmony. The
Lord enables marital success to those who lay down their lives in
submission to the biblical precepts of marital oneness (Ps. 25:14).
God is pleased with such sacrifice and bestows His covenant

blessings on those who love Him (Ps. 133:1). Couples die daily in humble service, where it increasingly becomes more blessed to give than to receive. The outcome is that they draw near to each other by self-sacrifice in ever-increasing marital intimacy:

- So then, brethren, we are under obligation, not to the flesh, to live according to the flesh—for if you are living according to the flesh, you must die; but if by the Spirit you are putting to death the deeds of the body, you will live (Rom. 8:12–13).

- You were taught, with regard to your former way of life, to put off your old self, which is being corrupted by its deceitful desires; to be made new in the attitude of your minds; and to put on the new self, created to be like God in true righteousness and holiness (Eph. 4:22–24).

Marriage Covenant is Mutual Belonging

A marriage covenant is a sacrificial offering of self for a lifetime. This act of exchange implies love in belonging. Jesus affirmed the concept of belonging in marriage when he said that the bride belongs to the bridegroom and the bridegroom belongs to the bride (Jn. 3:29). The bride in the Song of Songs declares this belonging, proclaiming: "My beloved is mine, and I am his" (Song 6:3).

This belonging also implies that all possessions that spouses own belong to each other. There is no withholding of self or possessions. Our Lord Christ Jesus exemplifies this. He asserted that he and the Father are one (Jn. 10:30). He further explained the nature of that oneness by claiming that all that belongs to the Father belongs to Him (Jn. 16:14).

God calls Christians his own, for we belong to Him (Jn.17:24). God accepts us with all our failings and weaknesses, for "while we were still sinners, Christ died for us" (Rom. 5:8). Likewise, husbands and wives come with personality wrinkles and character imperfections. Just as Christ's love was unconditional, so should a covenant husband and a wife's love be toward each other.

The Lord calls spouses to be gentle and patient, "bearing with one another in love," in their imperfections (Eph. 4:2). A covenant wife should honor her imperfect husband, reflecting God's love (Prov. 12:4). A covenant husband should imitate Christ and love his imperfect wife as Christ loves the Church (Eph. 5:25–28). God imparts his blessings through covenant. The most blessed marriages are those aligned with the kingdom principles of covenant marriage. The pathway of covenant marriage is in the pursuit of marriage oneness.

Chapter 4

The Divine Calling of Marriage
Representing Christ and the Church

*M*arriage begins in the spiritual realm and is expressed in the natural dimension over a lifetime. Marriage is a divine calling. Not everyone feels called to marriage (Matt. 19:11–12). All aspects of the Christian marriage are holy. Every purpose of the Christian marriage is sacred. God created marriage for love, companionship, comfort, mutual support, and intimacy (Gen. 2:18). Marriage is also for reproduction and the creation of the family for the continuity of godly generations (Eph. 6:4). God instructed Adam and Eve to "be fruitful and increase in number; fill the earth and subdue it" (Gen. 1:28). The Lord noted through the prophet Malachi the mystery of marital oneness. God also declared His desire that humans raise godly offspring from their union:

"Didn't the LORD make you one with your wife? In body and spirit, you are his. And what does he want? Godly children from your union" (Mal. 2:15, NLT, emphasis added).

The Ultimate Purpose of Marriage

The ultimate purpose of marriage is to bring glory to God by representing Christ and the Church (Eph. 5:21–33). The Church is the bride of Christ (Rev. 19:7). God uses his marriage relationship with His bride as a model for a husband and a wife to emulate (Eph.

5:21–33). God beseeches us to let our light shine before others that they may see our good deeds and glorify our Father in Heaven (Matt. 5:16). Jesus, in pray, told his Father that he gave the disciples the glory that he received from him, so "that they may be one just as we are one" (Jn. 17:22, emphasis added).

Born-again Christians are God's temple, for God's Spirit dwells within us (1 Cor. 3:16). The Tabernacle of God housed the glory of God in the Holy of Holies (Heb. 9:1–5). Christian couples as the temple of God carries his presence (the glory) through the indwelling of the Holy Spirit. In the same way, married couples reflect God's glory in the manifestation of the mystery of marital oneness. Couples realize fulfillment when they seek to live out God's precepts on marriage by following in the model of Christ's relationship with the Church.

Representing the Kingdom of Heaven on Earth

Jesus Christ came to earth preaching about the kingdom of Heaven and the means to enter through repentance and faith (Matt. 4:17). He prayed that his kingdom be established on earth as it is in Heaven (Matt. 6:10). God's ultimate purpose is to establish his kingdom in the world (Isa. 9:6–7). In this age, the Church of God represents his kingdom on earth. God has delegated his authority to the Church to influence the world by implementing kingdom principles. Christians are the light and salt of the earth in demonstrating these principles (Matt. 5:13–16).

The family is the foundational institution of society. Marriage is the door to the creation of the family. God has delegated his authority to husbands and wives to implement the order, precepts, laws, and principles of oneness in their marriages (Eph. 5:21–33). God has promised abundant blessings on marriage when couples embrace the culture of the kingdom of Heaven (Ps. 133:1–3).

As individuals, God wants couples to represent Him in loving each other. He gave humans his likeness and His Spirit. His attributes are seen in us. The Holy Spirit reflects the characteristics of God and thus glorifies him. Married couples express the glory of oneness as the Spirit gradually transforms us into the image of Christ:

"And we all, with unveiled faces, beholding the glory of the Lord, *are being transformed into the same image from one degree of glory to another. For this comes from the Lord who is the Spirit*" (2 Cor.3:8, ESV).

Creating the Heavenly Culture of Oneness on Earth

Christian couples are ambassadors of Christ. The Holy Spirit empowers Christians to exemplify the culture of unity on earth as it is in Heaven (Matt. 6:10). The culture in Heaven is perfect oneness (Jn. 10:30). God instructs Christian couples to showcase their marriage to the world as a witness of the culture of the heavenly kingdom, a portrait of Christ and the Church (Eph. 5:21–23, 32). Christ works through married couples to release the practice of married oneness (Gen. 2:240). Christ desires that couples reproduce Heaven's unity on earth, glorifying the Father in Heaven (Matt. 5:16).

Christian marriages should illustrate oneness reflecting Christ's relationship with his bride, the Church (1 Cor. 3:3). The Holy Spirit imprints his love on spouses' hearts, on their confession of faith in their vows, affirming their oneness. As the fruit of oneness is displayed, God is glorified (Jn. 15:8). God promotes oneness in spouses by giving them "the desire and the power to do what pleases him" (Phil. 2:13, NLT).

The Holy Spirit indwells Christians with his glory to enable unity in the Body of Christ. But this concept can also be applied to marriage:

> I have given them the glory you gave me, that they
> may be one as we are one—I in them and you in me—
> so that they may be brought to complete unity. Then
> the world will know that you sent me and have loved
> them even as you have loved me (John 17:22–23).

Pursuing oneness is the labor of love through a life of living out kingdom principles and precepts of marriage. Married couples that live by kingdom principles are advancing the culture of the kingdom of Heaven. God has prepared a unique work of marital oneness for each couple that he may fashion them together as his workmanship for his glory (Eph. 2:10). God's Spirit empowers and guides spouses to travel their unique path prepared for them to exhibit Christ's sacrificial love for the Church (Heb. 12:1).

Reflecting His Light

The Church is the bride of Christ, reflecting His light to the world. Jesus said, "I am the light of the world. Whoever follows me will never walk in darkness, but will have the light of life" (Jn. 8:12). But Jesus also maintains that we are the light of the world:

> You are the light of the world. A town built on a hill
> cannot be hidden. Neither do people light a lamp
> and put it under a bowl. Instead they put it on its
> stand, and it gives light to everyone in the house.
> In the same way, let your light shine before others,
> that they may see your good deeds and glorify your
> Father in Heaven (Matt. 5:14–16).

The apostle Paul outlines the foundational principles that would produce a fulfilling marriage. These articles, if you will, are the constitution for the marriage institution. The concepts of love, leadership, faithfulness, respect, sacrifice, submission, service, honor, devotion, and unity characterize the relationship between Christ and the Church (Eph. 5:21–33). These virtues are the cornerstone principles that reflect God's glory (1 Cor. 3:11–14).

Husbands and wives represent the love of Christ in the context of their union. God works out marital oneness by the Holy Spirit that lives through us (Phil. 2:13). We have been crucified with Christ, such that we no longer live, but Christ lives through us in the formation of married oneness (Gal. 2:20).

That the World May Know the Love of Christ

Christian couples are to reflect God's glory not only in the body of Christ but also to showcase Christ's love to the world (1 Tim. 3:7). God prioritizes unity in the Church. He prizes unity in marriage by exalting the marital relationship to the love relationship between Christ and the Church. Jesus used the principle of unity as a means by which the world would know God's love and believe the Gospel:

> My prayer is not for them alone. I pray also for those who will believe in me through their message, that all of them may be one, Father, just as you are in me and I am in you. May they also be in us so that the world may believe that you have sent me. I have given them the glory that you gave me, that they may be one as we are one—I in them and you in me—so that they may be brought to complete unity. Then the world will know that you sent me and have loved them even as you have loved me (Matt. 17:20–23).

Couples are to model the oneness of the Godhead to the world that they may know that God sent his Son to save the world (Jn. 3:16). The Holy Spirit lives in us to work out the elements of the marital union. We are not alone. Jesus Christ is our co-laborer in manifesting God's portrait of oneness through a husband and wife (1 Cor. 3:9). The Holy Spirit and the Christian couple are the threefold cord that works together to release the attributes of marital oneness God imparted at the altar. Love identifies Christians to the world (Jn. 13:35). Married couples uniquely display that love in their identity as one.

Expressing God's Will for Unity

Knowing and walking in God's will is to bring glory to God. God has marked out the path for Christians to find his will and for couples who seek to walk in oneness:

> Therefore, I urge you, brothers and sisters, in view of God's mercy, to offer your bodies as a living sacrifice, holy and pleasing to God—this is your true and proper worship. Do not conform to the pattern of this world, but be transformed by the renewing of your mind. Then you will be able to test and approve what God's will is—his good, pleasing and perfect will (Rom. 12:1–2).

When individuals conform to God's will, ever-increasing love is enabled. Married couples who live by faith in their oneness would see their union as a co-mission to express God's love like Christ's love for the Church. Spouses offer themselves as living sacrifices to each other, bringing glory to Him who gave the ultimate sacrifice to humanity.

When marriage is perceived as a portrait of the relationship between Christ and the Church, the pursuit of oneness becomes more compelling. This biblical worldview informs a couple's goals, plans, and decisions. Husbands and wives embrace their destiny as fulfilling God's plan for their lives. Spouses are Spirit-empowered and divinely purpose-driven (Eph. 2:6). Christian couples are enabled to express God's will of unity in representing the heavenly model (1 Cor. 2:16).

Fulfilling Your Unique Destiny as One

What is God's calling to married couples in general? When it is all said and done, does it matter how we lived our marriage? Is it our achievements that we might have the praises and admiration of society? Is it pioneering our path in pursuing our ambitions? Is it to discover and fulfill God's will for ourselves, our marriage, our children, and our ministry? Finally, are we laying up treasures on earth or in Heaven? (Matt. 6:19–21). All our success on this earth becomes ashes if it does not have significance for the kingdom of God (1 Cor. 3:12–14).

The answer to the forgone questions is to know God's common purpose for marriage and walk in it. But it is also to find God's unique destiny for your marriage union. What matters is if we lived faithfully after the pattern in the Word on marriage.

The Christian's destiny is to offer true worship by becoming a living sacrifice holy and pleasing to God (Rom. 12:1). Then we will be able to discover God's good, pleasing, and perfect will, tailored for our lives, in the unfolding mystery of marital oneness (Rom. 12:2). King Solomon was the wisest man who ever lived. After exploring the universe of life experiences, including having seven hundred wives, the monarch, under the inspiration of the Holy Spirit, concluded that the pathway to fulfillment is first pursuing oneness with God (Eccl. 12:13).

Chapter 5

The Foundation of Marriage
Jesus Christ Cornerstone

*M*ost Christian couples I counseled inadvertently assimilated critical aspects of the world's marriage culture. These couples did not intentionally adopt principles and practices for their marriage. Generally, they subconsciously conform to family and societal norms. Most couples learn by social modeling from family, media, and community in creating their marriage.

Like Lot in the city of Sodom, spouses can become so consumed by the world's culture that this lifestyle becomes the acceptable standard. Lot had become very familiar with the customs of Sodom. God sent angels to remove him and his family to safety. Lot hesitated such that the angels had to take him by the hand and move him out of the city. Lot's wife looked back longingly and became a pillar of salt (Gen. 19:15–26). Lot had become the proverbial frog in boiling water. The manner of life in Sodom had gradually desensitized him. Such is the case with married partners who consistently quarrel, fight, and struggle in their marriage. They primarily operate by the pattern of this world's system.

How Can We Sing the Lord's Song in a Strange Land?

There is a general disconnect between some Christian couples' beliefs and the fundamental principles of biblical marriage that ought to inform their lifestyle. As we previously discussed, the cultural habits that I found in counseling sessions are mostly not intentional. They result from subconscious thought patterns derived from the assimilation of family and societal practices. Our belief system generates our behaviors. You become what you believe (Prov. 23:7).

Here is an illustrative analogy that can help to explain the relationship between our thought patterns and our behavior. The Israelites were in captivity by the rivers of Babylon. Their captors asked them to sing to them one of the joyful songs of Zion. But the Israelites replied, "How can we sing the songs of the Lord while in a foreign land?" (Ps. 137:4).

Married couples have asked me, "Why are we not happy after trying so hard?" They lived in "Babylon's" psychological mindset in nearly all cases. These couples were operating under the marital principles of the world and not the Judeo-Christian precepts in the Word. They were in a "foreign land," unwittingly adopting the customs of the age. They were in captivity to the cultural belief system of the world. As Christians, they are citizens of Heaven but were not living by the governing principles of the kingdom of Heaven (Phil. 3:20). They were warring against the very sacred principles that are the foundation of marital peace and harmony.

Married couples cannot use self-effort and the carnal ways of the world system to find marital joy and happiness. Happy couples sing songs of joy in "the Lord's land." Couples must walk in biblical values and precepts to experience marital fulfillment. The ancient principles the Lord gave to Joshua in his generation are as prolific and enduring in contemporary society as it was then. Let the wisdom of the ancient words impart to you:

"Keep this Book of the Law always on your lips; meditate on it day and night so that you may be careful to do everything written in it. Then you will be prosperous and successful" (Josh. 1:8).

Sowing and Reaping in Marriage

The fundamental concept in pursuing oneness is faith in the marital union. Belief in oneness impels spouses to practice scriptural principles in their marriage. One such principle is sowing and reaping. God's Word asserts that people reap what they sow (Gal. 6:7). The prophet Hosea concurs that a person who sows to the wind will reap the whirlwind (Hos. 8:7). Deuteronomy chapter 28 details the many blessings for obedience to God's law and the curses for disobedience.

The principle of sowing and reaping has important implications for marriage. Living by the world's philosophies is sowing to the wind, even if the culture considers you a success. Couples who live by the world's standards will reap the works of the flesh. The actions of the flesh include envy, sexual immorality, jealousy, hatred, fits of rage, discord, dissensions, and selfish ambitions (Gal. 5:19–21). Conversely, sowing to the Spirit, living by the biblical truths on marriage, will harvest love, joy, peace, kindness, gentleness, self-control, and faithfulness (Gal. 5:22–23).

Sowing in the Spirit

On April 30, 1789, President George Washington gave his inaugural address to Congress. The president's words embody the biblical principles of sowing and reaping:

"The propitious smiles of Heaven can never be expected on a nation that disregards the eternal rules of order and right, which Heaven itself has ordained."

In the same vein, we can say:

"The propitious smiles of Heaven can never be expected on a marriage that disregards the eternal rules of order and right, which Heaven itself has ordained."

Marital success is conditional. God loves his children and wants to bless our marriages. However, he requires us to abide by His precepts on marriage to experience joy, peace, and happiness (Ps. 1). One cannot sow with worldly principles and reap the blessings of harmony and success that only come with believing in and living by the teachings of His Word on marriage (Ps. 1:1–3). Choosing to live by the righteous principles that govern marriage or the world's philosophies will determine the quality of your marital outcomes. Therefore, "sow righteousness for yourselves; reap the fruit of unfailing love" (Hos. 10:12).

The Foundation for Marital Success

I heard Dr. Tony Evans, pastor, and best-selling author, say: "Your foundation determines your future." I meditated on it. It emerged as a profound statement and is apt for our discussion here. So pause and ponder its meaning to marriage. I am not only referring to an acknowledgment of God as the foundation of marriage. Laying a foundation with the precepts and principles of covenant marriage under the headship of Jesus Christ is the only path to an enduring and fulfilling marriage.

Unless the Lord Builds the House

The quality of your marriage depends on its foundation. Our Lord Christ Jesus explained the principles of success or failure of human endeavors to their foundation. Our application is on the marriage institution. Jesus explained:

> Why do you call me, "Lord, Lord," and do not do what I say? As for everyone who comes to me and hears my words and puts them into practice, I will show you what they are like. They are like a man building a house who dug down deep and laid the foundation on rock. When a flood came, the torrent struck that house but could not shake it because it was well built. But the one who hears my words and does not put them into practice is like a man who built a house on the ground without a foundation. The moment the torrent struck that house, it collapsed, and its destruction was complete. (Lk. 6:46–49)

Married couples who follow the world's system build their house on sand. Their lifestyle is rooted in worldly philosophies and principles. They disregard the marital tenets of God, the very foundation of a successful marriage. Marital fulfillment is elusive to spouses whose life is informed by this world's philosophies and practices. The marriage structure cannot withstand the storm when conflicts and temptations arise. The relationship crumbles into continuous conflict, mere existence, or, at worst, divorce. Most of my clients pray, if not together, individually. They call on the Lord about their marital issues. Most of them have heard God's principles of marriage. Still, they build their house on the sand, the subliminal influence of family traditions and society.

The couple who hears and applies biblical precepts and principles to their marriage is like the man who dug down deep and laid the foundation on the rock in building his house. When the torrential floods came, the house was not shaken. These are the couples who submit to the headship of Jesus Christ in their marriage. They can withstand the storms of life that inevitably come. These couples do not have all the techniques and strategies to resolve every issue entirely. However, through faith in God and their oneness, they build on the marital principles, structures, precepts, and values in the Word of God.

Jesus is the Rock of our foundation. He is the author and finisher of our faith in the journey of marriage oneness (Heb. 12:2). The unions that prevail are the ones established on the Rock. Successful marriages are built by Jesus, for "unless the Lord builds the house, the builders labor in vain (Ps. 127:1).

Jesus Christ Cornerstone

The cornerstone concept in New Testament times is the first stone set in constructing a masonry foundation that orient the building in a specific direction. It was essential since all other stones were laid in reference to that stone. Builders placed the cornerstone as the foundation and standard for constructing a building. If the cornerstone were removed from a building, the entire structure would collapse.

Jesus is the Cornerstone of a successful marriage (Eph. 2:19–22). Spouses cannot experience authentic marital satisfaction apart from the one who founded the institution and wrote the manual for marriage success (Jn. 15:5). The love of Jesus for his bride is the portrait on which all enduring marital relationships are fashioned (Eph. 5:31–32).

Married couples can live out their marriage oneness with confidence in Christ, who began a good work at the altar and is faithful to carry it to completion (Phil. 1:6). Jesus not only died that we might have eternal life, but he lived in the flesh that we might have victory through his Spirit. Jesus Christ embodies the principles of Christian living. Since he lives in us, he expresses himself through our marriage (Gal. 1:15–16).

The Sufficiency of Scripture

After about three counseling sessions, some of my clients realize that their marriage is not rooted and grounded in the Word (Jn. 1:1). All the knowledge, wisdom, and understanding needed for a successful marriage is in the Word. The apostle Paul explains:

> My goal is that they may be encouraged in heart and united in love, so that they may have the full riches of complete understanding, in order that they may know the mystery of God, namely, Christ, in whom are hidden all the treasures of wisdom and knowledge (Col. 2:2–3).

The Holy Bible is the repository of all wisdom and understanding for a successful marriage (2 Pet. 1:3). All we need in the twenty-first century is embedded in the ancient truths of God's Word. The ancient Word still imparts. We can be confident that the Scriptures contain all the principles and precepts we need to have a successful marriage. There are direct instructions and implicit truths on marriage in the Word. These principles are riches to be mined through the Spirit. Such nuggets emerge by study and meditation of the Word (Ps. 1:1–3). Couples will discover that the ancient Word contains knowledge and precepts that apply to every contemporary situation and issue.

The Bible incorporates all the constitutional precepts and principles for success in all human endeavors:

- All Scripture is God-breathed and is useful for teaching, rebuking, correcting, and training in righteousness so that the servant of God may be thoroughly equipped for every good work (2 Tim. 3:16).

- Keep this Book of the Law always on your lips; meditate on it day and night so that you may be careful to do everything written in it. Then you will be prosperous and successful (Josh.1:8).

The Word of God contains all that spouses need to "be thoroughly equipped for every good work" in marriage (2 Tim. 3:17). The Holy Spirit quickens the Word for its current application. The ancient Word of the immutable God meets the ever-changing needs of the contemporary world. King David's declaration of the efficacy of God's Word for success and prosperity is enlightening:

> The law of the Lord is perfect, refreshing the soul. The statutes of the Lord are trustworthy, making wise the simple. The precepts of the Lord are right, giving joy to the heart. The commands of the Lord are radiant, giving light to the eyes. The fear of the Lord is pure, enduring forever. The decrees of the Lord are firm, and all of them are righteous. They are more precious than gold than much pure gold; they are sweeter than honey, than honey from the honeycomb. By them your servant is warned; in keeping them, there is great reward. (Ps. 19:7–11).

The Threefold Cord

When couples engage in spiritual disciplines together, they are cleaving to God as one. Couples are urged to cleave to each other but are exhorted to prioritize cleaving to God (Gen. 2:24). The foundation for marital success is to pursue oneness through God. Couples who cleave to God submit to His precepts on marriage and seek His will in fervent obedience (Deut. 30:20, Josh. 22:5). They abide in God as the branches are attached to the vine for their sustenance

(Jn. 15:1–17). Couples abide in God as they remain under God's love and protection, dwelling in "the shelter of the most high" (Ps. 91:1–3). Cleaving to God is a lifestyle of obedience and worship to Him and humble service to your spouse.

To abide in Christ means that God is first in the marital three-some. God's principles should prioritize every situation and decision (Matt. 6:33). God outlined the order of loving that is most rewarding to us. Jesus said that Christians should first love God followed by others (Matt. 22:37–40, Lk. 14:26). We cannot be one with our spouse without God first working out His love in us. We authentically love our spouse when we first love God. The apostle John confirms this truth:

"This is how we know that we love the children of God: by loving God and carrying out his commands" (1 Jn. 5:2).

Submitting to marital truths in your marriage affirms the triune nature of your marriage relationship. The centrality of Christ Jesus as "the way the truth and the life" in a couple's married life underscores the threefold nature of covenant marriage (Jn. 14:6). Spouses must live with the ever-present consciousness of the Holy Spirit as the marriage counselor, who leads them into all truth (Eccl. 4:12). The Holy Spirit in us releases the virtues of oneness (Phil. 2:13). Recognizing the triune nature of the Christian marriage is to establish in our hearts that our strength comes from the Lord:

> Two are better than one because they have a good return for their labor: If either of them falls down, one can help the other up. But pity anyone who falls and has no one to help them up. Also, if two lie down together, they will keep warm. But how can one keep warm alone? Though one may be overpowered, two can defend themselves. A cord of three strands is not quickly broken (Eccl. 4:9–12).

The threesome nature of marriage increases our faith, knowing that He who began the work of oneness at the altar is the head of the marital union (1 Cor. 11:3). Authentic love for one's spouse is predicated upon our relationship and fellowship with God. A submissive and intimate relationship with God produces an enduring love in marriage.

Marital Success Is Rooted in Relationship with God

In 2007–2008, the Barna Group conducted studies on divorce rates in America. The research found that Christians are just as likely to divorce as are non-Christians. The study further confirmed its findings through tracking studies conducted each year since that time.

Other studies have found that divorce rates differ significantly between nominal Christians and those who actively engage with their faith. Research reviewed on Focus on the Family asserts that the factors that make the difference in marriage longevity are religious commitment and practice. Such religious behaviors and attitudes include any combination of regular weekly church attendance, Bible reading, praying privately and together, and commitment to faith. The article summarized that Christian couples who practice such spiritual disciplines show significantly lower divorce rates than nominal Christians and unbelievers. The clinical research reported that couples who pray together regularly experience marital benefits such as increased forgiveness, emotional and sexual fidelity, trust, greater unity, and relational happiness.

Integrated Catholic Life reviewed a Gallup poll commissioned in 1997 by the National Association for Marriage Enhancement that concurs with the findings that couples who engage in spiritual activities significantly increase the prospect of marriage success.

The data showed that the divorce rate among couples who pray together was 1 out of 1,152. That is less than 1 percent!

Therefore, what conclusion can we draw? The evidence is clear. Couples who regularly and seriously engage in faith practices together, including Bible reading, prayer, reading and listening to material for spiritual growth, and church attendance, significantly increase their prospects for marital success. God's Word has made this truth abundantly clear (2 Tim. 3:16). Spiritual activities engender intimacy with God that transforms us more into the character of Christ. Spiritual renewal generates affection with your spouse. The more your life reflects the nature of Christ, the greater your capacity to serve and love your spouse (Gal. 2:20, Prov. 4:18).

Part 2

The Purity and Passion of Covenant Marriage:

The Pathway of Marital Intimacy

Chapter 6

The Spirit of Covenant Marriage
Sacrifice and Commitment

The Song of Songs: God's Portrait of Married Love

*T*he Song of Songs is the biblical book of poetry devoted exclusively to marital love. Hebrew sages refer to the Song of Songs as "the most excellent of all songs," implying married love's exclusive and consummate nature.

The Song of Songs celebrates beauty, grace, sacrifice, and sanctity with intense longing and belonging in the ultimate expression of courtship and marriage. The Song of Songs is also an allegory of God the Bridegroom and Israel the Bride in the Old Covenant. The New Covenant depicts Jesus the Bridegroom and His Bride the Church (Rev. 19:7).

The Song of Songs weaves a beautiful tapestry of the purity of love in all its forms. In breathtaking imagery, it incorporates sacrificial devotion, intimate friendship, romance, and sexual passion. The Song is the ultimate allegory depicting God's captivating love lived through the human spirit to pursue the mystery of marital oneness. The apostle Paul captures the essence of this mystery:

"For this reason, a man will leave his father and mother and be united to his wife, and the two will become one flesh. This is a profound mystery—but I am talking about Christ and the church" (Eph. 5:31–32).

The Song of Songs uses three Hebrew words to capture the all-encompassing breadth and depth of the meaning of love in marriage. The Hebrew words utilized are *ahava, raya,* and *dod. Ahava* is primarily unconditional and sacrificial love, *raya* is principally intimate friendship, and *dod* is essentially the sexual and romantic dimensions of marital love. Together these three aspects of matrimony define the wholeness of the fulfilled marriage.

These three facets of marital love are all interwoven in delivering the joy and happiness of married love. In this chapter, we will explore *ahava* love. *Ahava* love is the bedrock of marital love. The spirit of marriage depicts love as originating from the center of one's being from which all of life's expressions emanate. God's Word concurs that "a good man brings good things out of the good stored up in him, and an evil man brings evil things out of the evil stored up in him" (Matt. 12:35). The other two features of marital love, *raya,* and *dod* will be discussed in the following two chapters.

The Purity and Passion of Ahava Love

Ahava love is unconditional. At its core, it is sacrifice and commitment. *Ahava* love is not dependent on an object for its existence but is a state of being. *Ahava* love is not reliant on feelings. It is consistent and unyielding in its commitment. It is an intentional choice to love one's spouse as Christ loves the Church (Eph. 5:25). *Ahava* love is most intensely expressed in marriage when it is allied with intimate friendship and marital affection:

> Place me like a seal over your heart, like a seal on
> your arm; for love (*ahava*) is as strong as death,
> it's jealously unyielding as the grave. It burns like
> blazing fire, like a mighty flame. Many waters

cannot quench love (*ahava*); rivers cannot sweep it away. If one were to give all the wealth of one's house for love (ahava), it would be utterly scorned (Song 8:6–7, parentheses added).

Ahava *Love Is an Attribute of the Holy Spirit*

The Scriptures describe *ahava* love as an attribute that forms our character. Authentic love is, therefore, a part of your very being. The Word of God portrays love as character traits such as kindness, patience, humility, generosity, goodness, and trustworthiness. The apostle Paul articulated the meaning of *ahava* love to the Corinthians:

> Love is patient, love is kind. It does not envy, it does not boast, it is not proud. It does not dishonor others, it is not self-seeking, it is not easily angered, and it keeps no record of wrongs. Love does not delight in evil but rejoices with the truth. It always protects, always trusts, always hopes, always perseveres. (1 Cor.13:4–7)

These attributes are the fruit of the Spirit. *Ahava* love embodies the fruit of the Spirit. The more you surrender to Jesus Christ as Lord, the more you display God's love. The degree to which you bear the fruit of the Spirit positively correlates to your marital fulfillment.

What do couples most want from each other? Essentially, and overwhelmingly, they desire a spouse that reflects *ahava* love, the fruit of the Spirit. Couples want partners that are patient, kind, gentle, faithful, and self-controlled (Gal. 5:22–23). The nucleus of most marital problems is a cry for the expression of the fruit of the Spirit. A young couple came into counseling about marital conflict. The wife spoke for about forty minutes detailing the problem. I then asked the husband to tell his story and what he wanted out of the counseling. He answered "peace" and stopped there. His wife had already detailed the substance of the issue.

Ahava *Love Is an Act of the Will*

Ahava love is primarily an act of will and not emotions. It is sacrificial and unconditional. *Ahava* love embodies loyalty, devotion, and commitment to one's covenant partner in words and deeds. The lovers in the Songs of Songs effusively express kindness and jealous protection (Song 3:5), faithfulness and honor (Song 8:6), and trust and devotion (Song 8:7).

Deeds are the evidence of love (1 Thess. 1:3). Action is implied as Christians are called to "walk in love" (2 Jn. 1:6). The apostle John admonishes us that love should not only be in words "but in deed and truth" (1 Jn. 3:18).

The nature of love is made complete by actions (Jm. 2:22). The attributes of love generate actions that bless others. *Ahava* love in marriage is acting on the faith in the marriage union. A patient husband will manifest *ahava* love in long-suffering behaviors toward his wife. A kind wife will do acts of kindness for her husband. Couples who believe in their oneness are devoted to each other in the loving expressions of their being, in words and deeds. They honor one another above themselves (Rom. 12:10).

Ahava *Love Is Sacrifice and Commitment*

The concept of sacrificial love is twofold. The first is the commitment to lay down one's life unconditionally in honoring one another above self. *Ahava* love defines God's sacrifice on the cross (Jn. 3:16). Thus, it is the unconditional commitment of the self to God and spouse. It is a humble service to your spouse out of reverence to God.

The second aspect of sacrificial love deals with attachment. A life of *ahava* love births increased marital intimacy. As previously mentioned, the term "sacrifice" comes from the Hebrew word *korban*. *Korban* means to "draw near," which is the essence of the Hebrew meaning of sacrifice.

In the Old Covenant times, the Israelites offered sacrifices to cover the sins that separated them from God. The blood of animals cleared the way to allow them to draw near to God. In its perfect form, *ahava* is God's gift to us. He gave His only Son as the sacrificial Lamb to redeem us. We "were once far away" but "have been brought near by the blood of Christ" (Eph. 2:13). Thus, sacrificial love is intended to bring closeness, to increasingly bond couples in an enhanced intimate relationship.

Love never fails; it perseveres (1 Cor. 13:7). An ordinary meaning of love in Western culture is its association with emotions. In Hebrew thought, *ahava* love is sacrifice, commitment, and loyalty, with emotion as a by-product and not the substance. Our faith expressing itself through love generates a nature of sacrifice and commitment (Gal. 5:6, Jm. 1:13).

Giving Is the Heart of Ahava *Love*

The root word of *ahava* is *ahav*. *Ahav* means giving, nurturing, being devoted to another, and providing and protecting as a privileged gift. The apostle Paul affirms this definition of love as "the most excellent way" (1 Cor. 12:31). Paul, in his letter to the Ephesians, elucidates the meaning of *ahava* love:

Husbands ought to love their wives as their own bodies. He who loves his wife loves himself. After all, no one ever hated their own body, but they feed and care for their body, just as Christ does the church—for we are members of his body. (Eph. 5:28–30)

Giving is the essence of *ahava* love. *Ahava* is a sacrificial love that "always protects, always trusts, always hopes, and always perseveres"

(1 Cor. 13:7). *Ahava* love is not self-seeking but in humility values others above self in the spirit of giving (1 Cor. 13:5). It is in accord with the directive that husbands "love their wives, just as Christ loves the Church and gave himself up for her" (Eph. 5:25). In its maturity, ahava love embodies the truth that "it is more blessed to give than to receive" (Acts 20:35). There is, of course, a reasonable expectation of receiving in marriage, but it is not the focus of *ahava* love. Ahava is unconditional love.

It is an established truth that more authentic mutual giving equals increased marital intimacy. The marriage act of giving self begins at the wedding altar when the bride and the groom sacrificially pledge themselves to each other. The primary mode of giving self is the gift of self in physical, intellectual, social, emotional, and spiritual relationships.

Such giving includes spending time together, exhibiting patience, praying together, engaging in mutually agreeable activities and dates, and sharing conversation in edifying and encouraging one another. Giving of self is being actively present for your spouse. In such genuine experiences from the heart that couples experience satisfying engagement. Only giving of self produces the true bond of intimacy between a husband and a wife.

The secondary aspect of giving is the giving of possessions. The act of giving of one's earthly goods from the heart is an extension of one's self. The rich, young ruler in the Gospels is a typical example. "Rich" was one of the labels that described who he was. The young ruler asked Jesus how to obtain eternal life. Jesus told him to keep the commandments.

The young man responded to Jesus, saying that he had kept the commandments from his youth. Jesus tested him. He told him to sell all his possessions and give to the poor, thus demonstrating sacrificial love. He went away sorrowfully. His wealth had become a part of himself. His possessions were a part of who he was. He was rich. He was unwilling to give himself to love God with all his heart and love his neighbor as himself (Matt. 22:37).

Jesus uncovered the obstacle that stood in the way of the rich, young ruler receiving salvation. He was not willing to lay down himself (Matt. 16:24). The rich, young ruler was not prepared to sacrifice what had become a part of him, demonstrating the faith that would lead to *ahava* love. He was unwilling to embrace the heart of God through sacrificial giving and commitment. The young ruler's problem was spiritual. The answer to marital issues is essentially spiritual, of the heart. Authentic sharing of one's possession is a measure of giving of self, for to give without love profits nothing (1 Cor. 1:1–3). Couples find marital fulfillment by giving all to God first and then to their spouse. They exhibit the true love of marriage by giving themselves in the spirit of *ahava* love: covenant commitment and sacrifice.

Chapter 7

The Soul of Covenant Marriage
Intimate Friendship

As you recall from the previous chapter, the Song of Songs uses three Hebrew words, *ahava*, *raya*, and *dod*, to capture love's rich and complete meaning in marriage. We discussed *ahava* love in Chapter 6. We will now discourse on *raya* love. *Raya* in biblical Hebrew translates as "friend." Webster describes a friend as a person you like and enjoy being with. In marriage, *raya* love implies a warm attachment that is mutually rewarding. It is a friend ship characterized by emotional intimacy.

David and Jonathan had such a *raya* friendship (1 Sam. 18:3). Moses loved (*ahava*) God. But because of his face-to-face interaction to know God, he was also called a friend (*raya*) of God (Ex. 33:11). Abraham's relationship with God also earned him the title of being called a friend of God (Jm. 2:23). It appears that Jesus had a *raya* friendship with John. Jesus loved (*ahava*) all the apostles, but there was a special bond (*raya*) with John. Interestingly, it was John who recorded:

"Now there was leaning on Jesus' bosom one of his disciples, whom Jesus loved" (Jn. 13:23, NKJV).

True to character, it was "the other disciple, the one Jesus loved," that recorded for Usain Bolt the significant fact that he outran Peter to Jesus's tomb:

> Early on the first day of the week, while it was still dark, Mary Magdalene went to the tomb and saw that the stone had been removed from the entrance. So she came running to Simon Peter and the other disciple, the one Jesus loved, and said, "They have taken the Lord out of the tomb, and we don't know where they have put him!" So Peter and the other disciple started for the tomb. Both were running, but the other disciple outran Peter and reached the tomb first. (Jn. 20:1–4).

Friendship is an essential pillar of an enduring and fulfilling marriage. Empirical research reveals that intimate friendship between couples is one of the core factors in marital satisfaction and a strong indicator of marriage success. A close friendship between married couples nurtures spiritual, emotional, and physical intimacy. Covenant friends in marriage; like each other, commit to each other, trust each other, encourage each other, and open their hearts wide in words and deeds. Covenant spouses are intentional in building an intimate friendship.

Raya *Friendship Is Complementary*

Raya love is complementary, alluding to reciprocal companionship. In marriage, *raya* love is a friendship with mutual concern and affection, where each spouse seeks to serve and meet the others' needs.

When Adam was created, there was not a suitable companion for him. God said that it was not good for Adam to be alone, and He would make him a counterpart that was equal to him and that complemented him (Gen. 2:18). God created Eve. Adam and Eve, male and female, complemented each other according to God's plan (Gen. 5:2).

Raya *Friendship is Trust*

Raya love in marriage is a covenant friendship built on mutual trust (1 Cor. 137). A covenant relationship implies trust. Covenant partners believe in the best of each other's motives. It is a commitment that is rooted in lasting trust and loyalty. Covenant love in marriage begins with trust and continues in such faith. It is analogous to our salvation experience. We begin in faith and must live by faith (Rom. 1:17).

The first act in our relationship with God is trust. We have faith in God by His grace for our salvation before we begin the journey in divine love. Unlike natural human affection, God's love is unconditional. We were sinners when Christ died for us. Abraham was a friend of God because he trusted God:

"Abraham believed God, and it was credited to him as righteousness, and he was called a friend of God" (Jm. 2:23).

In the Song of Songs, the bride expresses her trust in her lover:

"Let him lead me to the banquet hall, and let his banner over me be love" (Song 2:4).

The banner alludes to protective care implying the bride's confident trust in the bridegroom's love and protection. Sometimes marriages are plagued with mistrust when one or both spouses are habitually mistrustful based on emotions and not factual evidence. A lack of trust is a significant barrier to intimate friendship.

Without faith, it is impossible to please God (Heb. 11:6). Without trust, it is impossible to find genuine intimacy with your spouse. I counseled a client who frequently responded to her husband's explanations with, "I don't believe you." I would then inquire what the basis for her objection was. She would calmly reply, "I just don't believe him." She acknowledged that her husband did not have a history of deceit and had no factual basis for mistrusting him.

Future sessions revealed that she had an early life of abandonment and disappointment as a child and late into her teens. Her response was not just to her husband but was a universal character trait. Such counseling issues require relational, cognitive therapy rooted in scriptural principles and precepts of faith and transformation. Trust is an essential factor in the spiritual growth of marriage intimacy.

Raya *Friendship Spells Respect*

Raya love is friendship that displays great honor and deep respect. Solomon expresses the purity of *raya* friendship with passion but with great respect. The connotation in Solomon's use of the word "sister" implies great honor paid toward his bride. The king communicates passionate love to his bride and at the same time conveys a deep respect for her as a sister:

> You have stolen my heart, my sister, my bride; you have stolen my heart with one glance of your eyes, with one jewel of your necklace. How delightful is your love, my sister, my bride! How much more pleasing is your love than wine and the fragrance of your perfume more than any spice! Your lips drop sweetness as the honeycomb, my bride; milk and honey are under your tongue. The fragrance of your garments is like the fragrance of Lebanon. You are a garden locked up, my sister, my bride; you are a spring enclosed, a sealed fountain (Song 4:9–12).

Raya *Friendship Means Knowing Your Spouse*

Raya love means knowing your spouse. Understanding your spouse requires sharing your heart with unguarded transparency. Our Lord Jesus exemplified this open-heart relationship with his disciples when he said:

"I no longer call you servants because a servant does not know his master's business. Instead, I have called you friends, for everything I have learned from my father I have made known to you" (Jn. 15:15).

But what does it mean to know your spouse? Knowing someone takes on a special meaning in the Hebrew language. We will examine "knowing" in the context of human relationships and particularly relations based on covenant marriage. First, let us reference some biblical examples of what it means to know someone and apply it to marital friendship.

The Scripture says that Adam knew his wife (Gen. 4:1). The Hebrew word "knew" is *yada* and describes an intimate relationship such as sexual intercourse. However, *yada* is not limited to the sexual experience but encompasses a broader meaning. Yada means to know through relational experience, not just having intellectual knowledge. The Scripture uses a different Hebrew word, *shakab*, to describe a sexual encounter devoid of spiritual and emotional attachment. Adam and Eve had a covenant marriage and an intimate friendship. *Yada* infers that Adam knew his wife, not only sexually but also shared a spiritual, social, intellectual, and emotional attachment.

Abraham had an intimate relationship with God. When God asked Abraham to sacrifice Isaac, he obeyed. God withheld the hand of Abraham, stopping him from slaying Isaac. God said, "Now I know that you fear God" (Gen. 22:12). God was not simply saying that he had acquired knowledge that Abraham feared God. God meant that He and Abraham had an interactional and powerful emotional and spiritual experience involving faith in action (Jm. 2:21–23). That experience revealed Abraham's character. *Raya* lovers in marriage know each other intimately through experience and are devoted to each other by covenant. Their faith in God's truth of oneness motivates them to interact in ways that foster intimate friendship.

God had many experiences with Moses. God summarizes His relationship with Moses, which gives us an insight into the depths of authentic friendship:

"He revealed his character to Moses and his deeds to the people of Israel" (Ps. 103:7, NLT).

Married couples must emulate Moses's relationship with God to attain true friendship and marital fulfillment. God showed many miraculous deeds to Moses and the Israelites. But additionally, God revealed His character and His ways to Moses.

Married partners who remain at the level of revealing their routine actions will only experience a surface relationship with their spouse. Transparent couples share heartfelt experiences in words and deeds. They share strengths, weaknesses, successes, failures, joy, and sorrow.

Raya *Friendship through Dating*

For the remainder of this discussion, we will explore some experiences that foster strong, affectionate, and devoted friendship in marriage. We will begin with dating. Spending quality time together in dating enables a bonding experience between couples. *Raya* lovers spend both quality and quantity time together. Staying connected through quality dating experiences promotes enduring friendship between married couples.

There is a saying that "absence makes the heart grow fonder." I believe absence may make the heart long for each other. I think it is presence that makes the heart go fonder. When spouses share mutually beneficial experiences, they grow fond of each other. Quality time together builds lasting friendships. Husbands and wives get to nurture affection and thus like each other more. This fondness grows into cherished friendship and strengthens marital commitment. Authentic friendship blossoms when a husband and a wife frequently date. Husbands and wives facilitate marital intimacy and create treasured memories by spending quality time together on romantic dates.

The lovers in the Song of Songs spent quality and quantity time romancing each other. Here Solomon addresses his wife:

> My beloved hath answered and said to me, "Rise up, my friend [*raya*], my fair one, and come away, for lo, the winter hath passed by, the rain hath passed away—it hath gone. The flowers have appeared in the earth, the time of the singing hath come, and the voice of the turtle was heard in our land, the fig-tree hath ripened her green figs, and the sweet-smelling vines have given forth fragrance. Rise, come, my friend [*raya*], my fair one, yea, come away. (Song 2:10–13, YLT, parentheses added)

Generally, husbands are expected to be assertive in leading their wives on dating adventures. Our societal norms largely seem to assent to this. The Song of Songs implies an additional perspective, where the wife frequently initiates the romance. The wife in the Song of Songs primarily articulates and initiates the romantic encounters. The wife in Songs expresses 60 percent of the romantic language and deeds. She also begins the Song of Songs (Song 1:1–3) and ends the poetic love story (Song 8:10–18). She pursues her husband with grace, gentleness, and elegance. She portrays a captivating charm with a prolific display of words in alluring seductiveness:

> Come, my love, let's go to the field; let's spend the night among the henna blossoms. Let's go early to the vineyards; let's see if the vine has budded, if the blossom has opened, if the pomegranates are in bloom. There I will give you my caresses. (Song 7:12–13, CSB)

The wife in the Songs is free-spirited, expressive, sensual, transparent, graceful, and a liberated romantic lover. We can infer that marriages can improve when wives initiate dating and courtship experiences unabashed, beyond contemporary norms. In my pastoral counseling experience, many couples have reported increased emotional intimacy when a passive spouse (male or female) begins to initiate dating encounters more frequently. I suggest that couples schedule their dating experiences. Otherwise, the cares of the world can drown out your social life. Some couples plan their dating life once a week, others once every fortnight, others once a month. It all depends on your marital season and the current circumstances of life.

Raya *Friendship through Communication*

Effective communication builds intimate friendships between married couples. Communication can be verbal, written, or sign language for those with disabilities. Emotional bonding is multifaceted. One of the most productive facets is conversation. It is the most common way to communicate the contents of the heart. Conversation shares the treasures of the heart (Matt. 12:35). Your spouse receives the contents of your heart in honest exchange (Lk. 6:45).

Authentic communication is transparent, sharing dreams, joys, success, failures, sorrow, strengths, and weaknesses. Such heartfelt conversation deepens affection and creates emotional bonding between spouses. Couples should commit to at least once a month to discuss their relationship. The apostle Paul in communication with the Corinthian Church exemplifies how transparency relates to affection:

> We have spoken freely to you, Corinthians, and
> open wide our hearts to you. We are not holding our
> affection from you, but you are withholding yours

from us. As a fair exchange, I speak as to my children-open wide your hearts also (2 Cor. 6:11–13).

Effective Communication

Effective communication enhances marital intimacy. It is profitable for couples to hone into improving their conversation skills. One such skill is the art of listening. To hear is not just to perceive sound. The Hebrew word for "hear" is *shema*, which means listening and responding or obeying. The Psalmist wrote:

"The righteous cries out, and the Lord hears them [hears with the heart]; he delivers [action response] them from all their troubles" (Ps. 34:17, parentheses added).

Jesus said that whoever has ears, let him hear. Jesus meant that those who listen with the heart should respond in obedience (Matt. 11:15). As a child, I remember my mother giving me instructions to do a task. Sometimes I would not immediately engage in the activity. She would then say to me, "Did you hear me?" I knew she was not referring to whether I perceived and understood her order. She was referring to the fact that I was not responding by obeying.

Likewise, in conversation, a married couple should attentively engage each other and respond accurately with clarity. Spouses should acknowledge understanding and reflect appropriate emotion and tone. Your response in conversation is first to affirm your spouse before speaking to the content (Prov. 18:3).

Another helpful skill in communication is to be present for your spouse. The Lord exemplifies being present with undivided attention, accentuating eyes and ears:

"The **eyes** of the Lord are on the righteous, and his **ears** are attentive to their prayer" (1 Pet. 3:12, emphasis added).

The Lord does not only listen with keen eyes and ears. He responds with empathy (Heb. 4:15). Spouses should know that their words have been accurately received and emotionally perceived.

They will then be satisfied that the contents of their heart have been understood and shared by their loved ones. The spouses that affirm each other foster warm and secure friendships.

Raya Friendship Compliments

One of the most supportive interactions between couples is compliments. Compliments affirm and validate your spouse. Compliments help you focus on the positive things of your partner, building harmony and well-being in the marriage. God puts great value on compliments, and so should we. The following are some examples from the Lord's heart:

- "Kind words are like honey- sweet to the soul and healthy for the body" (Prov. 16:24, NLT).

- "Anxiety weighs down the heart, but a kind word cheers it up" (Prov. 12:25).

- Solomon to his wife: "How beautiful are you, my darling [raya]! How beautiful! Your eyes are like doves" (Song 1:15, NLT, parenthesis added).

- Wife to Solomon: "You are so handsome, my love, pleasing beyond words" (Song 1:16).

Friendship with God

A more intimate friendship with God enhances your capacity for a closer relationship with your spouse. The depth of intimacy between you and your spouse is positively related to your friendship with God. The primary way to receive revelation from God and thus draw closer to him is through the spiritual disciplines. These include Bible study and meditation, prayer, and worship. God wants to speak to you through these media. And He is personal. He calls your name when he communicates with you, as He did with Samuel, Abraham, Paul, and others (Jn. 10:3).

Friendship with God means submitting and loving God with all your heart, mind, and soul. It is the primary purpose of Christian living. Loving God brings the ultimate fulfillment to the human spirit. The human spirit could only find satisfaction in God. Then and only then can you authentically love your spouse with joy. Fellowship with God means that your life reflects the fruit of the Spirit. The fruit of the Spirit, love, joy, peace, kindness, goodness, faithfulness, patience, and gentleness, enhances the path to intimate friendship with your spouse.

The Bible is the primary source of building friendship with God. There are many excellent Bible-based books with scriptural insights, wisdom, and understanding that can inform you in navigating the journey of experiencing God at ever-greater depths and heights of intimacy. Three resources that have been a blessing to me are *The Pleasure of His Company: A Journey to Intimate Friendship with God*, by best-selling author Dutch Sheets, *Touching the Heart of God*, by best-selling author Paul Wilbur, and the best selling devotional, *My Utmost for His Highest* by Oswald Chambers. They are listed in the bibliography.

Chapter 8

The Joy and Pleasures of Covenant Marriage
Sex and Affection

*S*ex and affection in marriage are sacred gifts that a husband and a wife share in the spirit of humility and devotion (Rom. 12:10). The sexual union epitomizes the beauty of married oneness contained in the Song of Songs: "I am my beloved, and my beloved is mine" (Song 6:3).

One of the blessings of marriage is sexual fulfillment. God desires that a husband and wife enjoy the pleasures of sexual relations with each other:

"May your fountain be blessed, and may you rejoice in the wife of your youth. A loving doe, a graceful deer—may her breasts satisfy you always, may you ever be intoxicated with her love" (Prov. 5:18–19).

The above passage addresses the husband, but sexual satisfaction applies to both husband and wife. The intent is that both spouses rejoice, be mutually intoxicated with each other's love, and be blessed.

Joy and Pleasures of Sexual Intimacy

Sexual fulfillment is both pleasure and joy. Sexual pleasure is physical gratification. Sexual pleasure includes intimate physical and verbal affection and sensual stimulation that lead to the ecstasy of sexual orgasm. Sexual pleasure in a covenant marriage nurtures the body and soul.

Joy in this context signifies the delight of the spirit and the comfort and contentment of the soul. The spirit delights where there is a pure conscience (1 Pet. 3:16). The soul rejoices when there is peace of mind and emotional harmony (Phil. 4:7). Joy results from moral purity and mental and emotional well-being related to the sexual experience (Lk. 1:47).

The intensity of joy in marriage emanates from the intimacy, security, and purity experienced in the relationship. Joy in sex is complete when spouses love each other (*ahava*) and like each other (*raya*). The joy of sex at its origins is of the spirit. The source of joy is the Holy Spirit:

"There I will go to the altar of God, to God—the source of all my joy. I will praise you with my harp, O God, my God!" (Ps. 43:4).

Sexual joy comes when couples have purity, relational security, and emotional intimacy in their relationship. Joy in sex is thus the outcome of the grace of the Lord Jesus Christ in sustaining moral integrity, the love of God in enabling covenant commitment, and the fellowship of the Holy Spirit in nurturing marital friendship.

Sexual fulfillment is a function of physical pleasure, the emotional comfort and contentment of the soul, and peace through the sanctity of the spirit. Most spouses in my counseling experience, primarily but not exclusively wives, maintain that the joy of the sexual relationship is desired as much as the pleasures of making love.

Dod: *Romance and Sexual Passion*

We explored two components of marital love from the Song of Songs in the preceding two chapters: *ahava* (sacrifice and commitment) and *raya* (intimate friendship). The Hebrew word *dod* encapsulates the third aspect of married love. *Dod* love depicts the sphere of marital relationship of physical and emotional passion.

The Cambridge English Dictionary defines romance as the feeling of comfort and pleasure one experiences in a relationship with a loved one. Solomon's wife manifested romantic love when she exclaimed, "My heart began to pound for him" (Song 5:4). She was in love. Most people fall in love through the lover's physical appearance and personality. However, some couples have fallen in love gradually through deep admiration of appealing character traits that have created an attractive persona. Falling in love can be any combination of relationship experiences, physical attraction, character traits, and personality chemistry.

Romantic love is the thrill and appeal when you have dove's eyes for the loved one. One cannot adequately explain why a husband is captivated by his wife's eyes or smile; or why the tone of his voice can ignite a flame in her heart. A young couple can talk for two hours and feel that they were together for just twenty minutes. Similarly, couples in their silver years can sit silent as their hearts communicate in blissful peace, oblivious of time. One of my counselor associates called such quiet times "soaking love."

It is the thrill and mystery of romance, the zeal of young lovers, and the mellow passions of the golden years. The Song of Songs portrays marital romance in vivid imagery. When the purity of romance and sex synergizes with the covenant love of marital commitment and intimate friendship, they become a sacred flame.

Dod love manifests emotional and physical intimacy. This love includes physical and emotional attraction, romance, sex, and affection (Gen. 24:67, 26:7–9). The Song of Songs beautifully portrays *dod* love in the beauty and purity of romance and sexual passion. In the following passages, the bride and groom rhapsodize about each other in passionate *dod* form:

- "Let him kiss me with the kisses of his mouth—for your love [dod] is more delightful than wine" (Song 1:2, parenthesis added).

- "How delightful is your love [dod], my sister, my bride! How much more pleasing is your love [dod] than wine and the fragrance of your perfume more than spice! Your lips drop sweetness as the honeycomb; milk and honey are under your tongue. The fragrance of your garments is like the fragrance of Lebanon (Song 4:10–11, parentheses added).

- "My beloved *[dowdi]* is to me a sachet of myrrh resting between my breasts" (Song 2:16, parenthesis added).

- "My beloved *[dowdi]* thrust his hand through the latch-opening; my heart began to pound for him" (Song 5:4, parenthesis added).

- "His left arm is under my head, and his right arm embraces me... I am a wall, and my breasts are like towers. Thus, I have become in his eyes like one bringing contentment" (Song 8:3,10).

Sex: A Continuing Debt of Love

Sex between covenant partners is an "outstanding" and "continuing debt to love one another" (Rom. 13:8). *Dod* love infers knowing your mate intimately. As we previously discussed, the Hebrew word for "know" is *yada*. In the Scriptures, yada describes the sexual experience (Gen. 4:1). It results from a relationship of commitment and warm friendship in a covenant marriage. We are to love our spouse "according to knowledge," which suggests we must seek to know them intimately (1 Pet. 3:7, KJV).

The Scripture uses a different Hebrew word to describe a sexual act outside of a covenant relationship. The term *shakab* characterizes sexual encounters such as adultery (Deut. 22:22, 2 Sam. 11:4), fornication (Ex. 22:16), or rape (Gen. 34:2). Such sexual activity only results in perverted pleasure devoid of the joy of sexual fulfillment. It leaves the soul hungering. Sex in an authentic covenant love relationship satisfies the spirit, soul, and body

Marital Affection

Marital affection is a heartfelt gift in affirming words and touch shared by partners. It is not a list of actions that partners mechanically practice. Affection is custom-made. You must explore, know, and fully embrace the personality and character of your spouse so that your affection becomes a gratifying response from the heart to their unique character and personality. Spontaneous or intentional, God's love in our hearts works out in our display of affection (Rom. 5:5; Phil. 2:12). Solomon's wife paints a poetic picture of marital affection:

"Let's go early to the vineyards; let's see if the vine has budded, if the blossom has opened, if the pomegranates are in bloom. There I will give you my caresses" (Song 7:12, CSB).

Expressing affection in marriage is influenced by nature and nurture, personality, culture, and family upbringing. Affection is a natural disposition for some people. It is a learned behavior for others. Learning to express affection is sacrificial love (*ahava*) and friendship (*raya*) generating romantic love (*dod*). Over time the acquired behaviors become a natural disposition that will be gratifying to both partners (Acts 20:35).

Great lovers show affection in words and touch at all seasons, not only in sexual situations. They share heartfelt selfless expressions with their partner, turning ordinary moments into treasured memories. Affection nourishes the body and soul for a holistic sexual experience.

Marital Affection and Gender

Empirical studies reveal that females are generally more expressive with their affection than men. The Lord explicitly reminds husbands to love their wives. Such love includes marital affection (Eph. 5:5). The following scripture suggests that wives have a greater capacity and need for affection than men:

"Similarly, you husbands must live with your wives in an understanding manner, as with a most delicate partner. Honor them as heirs with you of the gracious gift of life so that nothing may interfere with your prayers" (1 Pet. 3:7, ISV).

Men in Western countries generally deemphasize affection. Men are typically not emotionally transparent as compared to women. Thus, some husbands have struggled with expressing affection in marriage. The husband's hesitancy to be generous with affection is mainly due to personality and acquired habits from family upbringing and cultural assimilation.

Generally, all husbands and wives desire to be loved by their spouses. Men's need for love from their wives is sometimes covert. I have counseled and coached hundreds of men over the last two decades. Men do desire and want the security of their wife's love. The apostle Paul affirmed that need to be highly essential when he urged older women to educate young women on how to love their husbands in meeting that need (Titus 2:4).

Most men, as most women, define love as meeting needs and wants, whether it is affection, sex, or other. Just as Adam, there was an innate desire for love and companionship (Gen. 2:18). That has not changed. The heart's ultimate need is love. The Song of Songs describes love as strong as death (Song 8:6). Interestingly, the Hebrew word that describes love here is *ahava*, the love of covenant commitment and sacrifice.

God's Manual on Marital Sex

Sexual satisfaction comes from giving self in mutually sharing physical pleasures. Sex is sacrifice in the context of the Hebrew meaning. The root meaning of sacrifice is "to draw near." Sex gives one's best gift or offering of self to draw near physically and emotionally. God created men and women with the capacity to love through relationships. Sexual pleasure is a bonding experience that enhances relationships and strengthens marital commitment.

The Word of God has given married couples some foundational precepts and principles to regulate and bless their sexual experience. God also provided the governing principles, responsibilities, and instructions for a mutually fulfilling sex life in marriage.

Mutual Submission out of Reverence for Christ

God's instructions on sex translate into expressions of love and affection between a husband and a wife who "submit to one another out of reverence to Christ" (Eph. 5:21). Marrieds give "preference to one another in honor" (Rom. 12:10). Spouses can fully live out God's counsel on sex and affection by embracing His marital precepts. The Holy Spirit enables them to share their sexuality with love rooted and established in Christ (Eph. 3:17).

Many of my clients argue about sex when the solutions are clearly in the Scriptures. My response is to redirect them to resolve the matter by searching into the book of the One who wrote the manual on sex. There is usually a quick agreement and realization that the buck stops with the Creator of sex.

God's Instructions on a Good Sex Life

We will now explore what God says about a good sex life in marriage. The following is the apostle Paul's counsel to married couples:

> **3** A husband should fulfill his marital responsibility to his wife, and likewise a wife to her husband.
>
> **4** It is not the wife who has the rights to her own body, but the husband. In the same way, it is not the husband who has the rights to his own body, but the wife.
>
> **5** Do not deprive each other, except by mutual agreement for a specific time, so that you may devote yourselves to prayer. Then resume your relationship so that Satan may not tempt you because of your lack of self-control. (1 Cor. 7:3–5, NET)

ERMA

To assist my clients in better understanding and embracing the apostle Paul's teachings on sex and affection in 1 Corinthians 7, I coined the phrase "Equal Rights Marriage Act," using the acronym ERMA. Please take note that these biblical directives are in the context of a normal relationship under natural circumstances. For example, I am not discussing sex in the light of such situations where there is illness or relationship dysfunction such as spousal abuse, addictions, or significant mental and emotional disorders.

Sexual Rights

Paul begins in 1 Corinthians 7:3 by saying that the husband should give his wife her sexual rights, referring to it as his marital responsibility. I do not think Paul was referring to having sexual intercourse per se with your wife. Most men generally do not have to be reminded of that. Paul was speaking about a qualified sexual experience that amounts to sexual fulfillment. Paul continues that the wife should give her husband his sexual rights. It is a marital obligation and a mutual debt of love (Rom. 13:8).

God's directive states that sexual relationship is an equal rights issue and not a privilege that one partner gives or withholds at will. Covenant marriage prescribes that a husband and wife have equal sexual rights as lovers. The Creator bestowed these rights as a gracious gift to married partners. Covenant marriage activates this principle.

Paul goes on in verse 4 to further comment on sexual rights concerning the bodies of a husband and a wife. The Word of God states that a husband does not have the rights or authority over his own body but yields it to his wife. Likewise, the wife surrenders herself to her husband.

Mutual Agreement

In 1 Corinthians 7:5, spouses are instructed not to deprive each other except by mutual agreement to spend time in prayer. According to God's order, having regular sexual relations is the standard order of the day (or night) in a marriage relationship. It is a continuing debt of love.

The decision not to engage in sex for a specified time is a joint decision of husband and wife and not a unilateral determination. Biblical directives imply that consent is a settled issue in sexual relations in covenant marriage. A discussion would ensue to arrive at a mutual agreement only when one partner presents a reason not to engage in sexual intercourse. This situation is the exception in Paul's counsel. The Word of God does not leave room for arbitrary individual decisions on sex on the part of one spouse in a covenant marriage, whether that be a husband or wife (1 Cor. 7:3–5). Recognizing this conjugal principle communicates to your spouse that you care and respect them and are faithful to your marriage covenant.

Finally, Paul urges couples in verse 5 not to have extended times of being apart sexually but to resume normal sexual relations, lest Satan brings temptation at an opportune time. The apostle Paul admonishes husbands and wives to regularly meet the sexual needs of each other to avoid temptation from Satan.

Loving Your Spouse Is Caring for Yourself

The truth that husbands and wives belong to each other is in the context of the following verse, which exemplifies the love of Christ:

> Husbands ought to love their wives as their own bodies. He who loves his wife loves himself. After all, no one ever hated his own body, but they feed and care for their body, just as Christ does the Church (Eph. 5:28–30).

The truth, of course, applies to both husband and wife. As elsewhere in Scripture, the husband represents the union as the leader in modeling godly behaviors. Therefore, Ephesians 5:28–30 could read:

"Wives ought to love their husbands as their own bodies. She who loves her husband loves herself. After all, no one ever hated his own body, but they feed and care for their body, just as Christ does the Church."

Let us recapitulate. The apostle Paul gave guidance to married couples on their sexual responsibility and debt of love to each other. He discussed each partner's rights to each other's body, joint decision-making on refraining from sex and ensuring the frequency of sexual relations. Ephesians 5 outlines the frame of reference from which all of Paul's instructions should apply. The context is to love your spouse as you love your own body, for those who love their spouse love themselves.

When a spouse accepts that they are one with their partner, they regard their sexual needs and desires as their very own. The apostle Paul explains sexual relations from this position of married oneness. Husbands and wives should wholeheartedly meet the sexual needs of each other as a continuing debt of love. This love engenders mutual benefit for husbands and wives in their marriage. Spouses that follow God's counsel on sex enhance the well-being of their own body, soul, and spirit and nurture their marriage relationship into greater joy and happiness (Eph. 5:28).

Chapter 9

Her Sexual Fulfillment
His Continuing Debt of Love

Fulfilling Her Needs

*G*od created women and men with some naturally different needs and responses to sex. God devised these contrasts that require sacrificial acts of love. These differences serve as a privileged opportunity for couples to demonstrate selfless caring in loving each other. Our discussions address the generalizations about the characteristics of the sexes. There are, however, always exceptions to the norm.

The Word instructs husbands to "love their wives as their own bodies, for he who loves his wife loves himself" (Eph. 5:28). Meeting sexual needs is one aspect of the Lord's counsel to husbands. For a husband to bring sexual satisfaction to his wife would include understanding female sexuality. It also involves discovering his wife's unique sexual needs and responses to please and pleasure her.

See Sex from Her Perspective

Some husbands generally tend to see sex from their gender perspective, not recognizing the distinctive needs of their wives. Sometimes wives accuse their husbands of not caring. But I have found from my counseling experience that most Christian husbands care. Usually, that is why they are in counseling. However, they may not have experienced a change from intellectual knowledge to emotional awareness regarding their wife's sexual needs.

Wives typically desire that their hearts be taken care of first before sharing the physical pleasures of the body. Wives generally want physical affection and verbal intimacy for an optimum sexual experience. Pleasing her is an expression of your being. It is good to learn the art of lovemaking, but it becomes complete with the art of love. It would then be a smooth transition from pleasuring her to pleasing her for a holistic and gratifying sexual experience of spirit, soul, and body.

Great sex does not begin in the bedroom. A wife's relationship with her husband outside the bedroom significantly affects her sexual satisfaction. That includes working habitually alongside your wife in household activities and childcare. As we previously mentioned, women generally possess a greater desire for physical affection and verbal intimacy than men. In the Song of Songs, Solomon's spouse consistently expresses her need for his affection:

- "Let him kiss me with the kisses of his mouth—for your love *[dod]* is more delightful than wine" (Song 1:2, parenthesis added).

- "His left arm is under my head, and his right arm embraces me...

- I am a wall, and my breasts are like towers.

- Thus I have become in his eyes like one bringing contentment" (Song 8:3,10).

Husbands who express kindness and affection regularly to their wives are more likely to create a fulfilling sexual experience than those who do not. When husbands share affection from the heart, it allows wives to experience sex holistically: the ecstatic pleasures of the body, the peace of spirit, and the comfort and contentment of the soul.

Her Emotional Readiness

Sex may satisfy the body but still leave the soul wanting. Justin and Jane (not their real names) illustrate this condition. They are two millennials in their late twenties. My perception is that they both genuinely love each other. During one of our discussions on sex, Jane turned to Justin and said:

"I want you to sometimes make love to me… (pause), just sometimes."

Justin, somewhat puzzled, replied: "Don't I?"

Jane responded: "No, you make love to my body. We have sex. My heart is still hungry. Just take some time to love **me** (Jane emphasized "me"). Pause to look into my eyes."

Justin, perplexed but concerned, replied: "What?"

That opened up the conversation to explore the concept of affection in marriage and what constitutes sexual fulfillment versus sexual pleasure. Our discussion revealed that Jane had the pleasure but no joy in their sexual encounters. There was no fulfilling emotional attachment to Justin. We discovered that Justin was unaware of Jane's need for heartfelt affection. Jane was confident of Justin's sincere but unexpressed love for her. In Justin's focus on physical pleasure (for both of them), he missed connecting with the person. When your wife feels both cared for and pleasured, the outcome is sexual gratification.

Her Emotional Attachment to Him

Jane's search was actually for the security of Justin's heartfelt expression of unconditional love. Jane knew Justin loved her but yearned for the practical assertion of his heart in words and deeds. Jane desired a more profound emotional attachment with him. She wanted a fusion of the physical act of sex and Justin's heart for a more meaningful and fulfilling sexual experience. One of my colleagues would sometimes say, "I feel you," to convey that she emotionally received someone's thoughts. This quote expresses what I believe Jane desired to communicate to Justin. She wanted an emotional connection. It is noteworthy to mention that the great love story of the Song of Songs describes love to be as strong as death. The preferred word used by the bride to express this love is *ahava*, the unconditional love of commitment and sacrifice. Ahava love is the foundational concept of love that authenticates the sexual experience.

Her Physical Readiness

As counseling progressed, Justin became more sensitive that Jane's sexual response was significantly different and required him to reexamine his sex life. He always knew but now had become emotionally aware. Justin's awareness prompted him to read a booklet on female sexual anatomy.

Justin became more mindful of Jane's need for physical and emotional readiness to enhance her sexual joy and pleasure. In the following two months, he revived his sex life. Jane announced humorously in one of their sessions, "He discovered me." Justin learned more about his wife's sexual anatomy and the need for physical and emotional readiness to enhance the joy and pleasures of their sex life. He had to take some tender loving time "to find her" the optimal joy and pleasures of sex, originating from his heart.

Pleasing Her

Creating a romantic ambiance in the bedroom enhances the joy and pleasure of sexual intimacy. Some women are sexually aroused by their husband's masculine fragrance as the wife of Solomon expressed her delight and appreciation:

"Pleasing is the fragrance of your perfumes; your name is like perfume poured out. No wonder the young women love you!" (Song 1:3).

Wives generally are emotionally and physically incited by compliments and words of endearment from their husbands. The wife of the Songs declared her joy about the tender and loving words of her husband:

"My beloved spoke and said to me, 'Arise, my darling, my beautiful one, come with me'" (Song 2:10).

Solomon also pours lavish praise on his wife, pleasing her abundantly and fostering the security of their love and well-being (Song 7:1–9).

Husbands tend to be sexually aroused by sight more quickly than wives. However, women do appreciate the attraction of the male physique, and Solomon's wife confirms that:

My beloved is radiant and ruddy, outstanding among ten thousand. His head is purest gold; his hair is wavy and black as a raven. His eyes are like doves by the water streams, washed in milk, mounted like jewels. His cheeks are like beds of spice, yielding perfume.
His lips are like lilies dripping with myrrh.
His arms are rods of gold set with topaz.
His body is like polished ivory decorated with lapis lazuli.
His legs are pillars of marble set on bases of pure gold.
His appearance is like Lebanon, choice as its cedars.
His mouth is sweetness itself; he is altogether lovely.

This is my beloved; this is my friend, daughters of Jerusalem. (Song 5:10–16)

Pleasuring Her

As Solomon's wife asserts, husbands should know that wives appreciate their bodies when they care for them. Wives value body massages with her unique scented aroma, slow and easy touch, and deep muscle caress. Yours to discover; mutual is the pleasure. A lovers' massage is not only a physically pleasurably experience but is an emotionally powerful bonding act of love between spouses.

The erogenous zones are the key to a wife having a truly ecstatic sexual rendezvous. Erogenous zones are sensitive areas of the body that elicit a pleasurable sexual response from both husband and wife when stimulated by a spouse's tender or vigorous touch. To be delicate or hearty is yours to discover which and when. Discover your wife's erogenous zones or sweet spots beyond the obvious ones such as breast and nipples, mouth, lips, and vagina.

Discoveries can present fresh opportunities for mutually heightened sexual ecstasy. One highly sensitive area is the clitoris, the premier sweet spot of female arousal and response. Sexologists name over 15 sensitive areas in the female sexual anatomy. I have refrained from listing them. It is your thrill to discover and for both of you to be pleasured.

Although some generally accepted erogenous zones may apply to women, every wife is unique in her sexual behavior to intimate touch in some areas. Besides naturally affirming responses, husbands and wives should communicate and explore to establish a mutual agreement in pleasuring each other. She will appreciate it. It is not within the scope of this discussion to give details on the subject of erogenous zones. Many good Christian books adequately address the topic.

Spend Some Time

Spending quantity and quality time to bring sexual satisfaction to your wife may be your most significant act of love in your physical union. Begin by learning the art and science of female sexual arousal and emotional response in general and your spouse's uniqueness. God created the female sexual anatomy to work much slower than the male. It allows the husband to exercise patience, understanding, and tender care in cherishing his wife. The vaginal area must be ready for a wife to experience optimal sexual pleasure. The vaginal area releases an arousal fluid for lubrication that bathes and protects the vaginal canal, allowing for penile penetration with ease and mutual pleasure. The vagina walls and clitoris swells in preparation for a more intense orgasm with adequate time. Spend some time.

Sexual Oneness

Couples find sexual fulfillment when sex goes beyond physical pleasure to the joy and contentment of spirit and soul. The result is greater unity and security in the marriage. In such bonding experiences, the Spirit of God advances the ever-evolving mystery of marital oneness.

Several studies have reported that increased sexual satisfaction is linked positively with better moods, job satisfaction, and greater work production. Research has also found a circular effect between sex and genuine verbal and physical affection. When husbands selflessly share more love and affection, wives become more amorous, increasing sexual engagement. When wives are amenable to more frequency in sexual activity, husbands tend to become more affectionate. This cycle generally leads to spouses sharing a warm, positive regard toward each other, generating greater marital intimacy. This sequence strengthens friendship and commitment toward maturing marriage oneness.

Chapter 10

His Sexual Fulfillment
Her Continuing Debt of Love

Fulfilling His Needs

*G*od created men and women with some naturally different needs and responses to sex. God devised these contrasts that require sacrificial acts of love. These differences serve as a privilege for couples to demonstrate selfless caring in loving each other. Our discussions address the generalizations about the characteristics of the sexes. There are, however, always exceptions to the norm. The Word instructs wives to learn "to love their husbands" (Titus 2:4). Meeting sexual needs is one aspect of the Lord's counsel wives. A wife can be better prepared to meet that need by learning about male sexuality and her husband's specific sexual needs and responses.

See Sex from His Perspective

Some women generally tend to view sex from their gender perspective, not recognizing the distinctive needs of their husbands. Sometimes husbands accuse their wives of not caring. But I have found from my counseling experience that most Christian wives generally care. Usually, that is why they are in counseling. However, they may not have experienced a change from intellectual knowledge to emotional awareness regarding their husband's sexual needs.

How a wife expresses love to her husband would depend partly on how she perceives his needs. Wives may perceive their husbands as needing physical pleasure or physical-emotional satisfaction. A wife's definition of her husband's sexual fulfillment would shape the measure of her response to him.

Most of my clients rarely introduce sex as their presenting issue, even when sex is the problem. Sexual issues usually emerge during counseling. A young couple, John and June (not their real names), came for counseling regarding some marital conflict issues. Somewhere in the conversation, the issue of sex emerged. June was consistently making the same excuse for not having sex. The reason June gave when John initiated sex; was that she did not feel like it.

I recognize that there could be several underlying reasons for June's response, but I took it at face value. Before we discussed the biblical precepts on sex or probed into the couple's relationship, I related a scenario to June that went like this:

Suppose you told John to warm up a slice of pizza for you, adding that you were hungry. John responded that he was not acceding to the request because he did not feel like eating pizza. June responded that John would be acting ridiculous. We discussed the issue of being responsive to our partner's needs from the partner's perspective. June later acknowledged that she had an increased understanding of John's sexuality and could better understand his needs

His Emotional Readiness

Respectful communication and honorable recognition of a husband's biblical role by his wife motivates him to greater sexual desire and passion for her. Some husbands tend to view sex as only a physical act when this is not so. I have counseled and coached hundreds of husbands who essentially shared that position. The Lord specifically says that a wife must respect her husband. Respect is a motivating factor for a husband toward a holistic sexual experience (Eph. 5:33).

The perspective from which wives view their husbands regarding their sexual needs is crucial in their sexual fulfillment. It is an issue of honor and respect for husbands. A wife's understanding will affect her response in meeting her husband's sexual needs. For example, some wives have asserted in counseling that sex for their husbands is essentially a one-dimensional experience, that being the physical realm.

Some husbands have accepted this characterization and act accordingly. Husbands who live within the reality that sex is only a physical act will experience an emotional void that sometimes makes them more likely susceptible to sexual temptation than a husband who shares a holistic sexual relationship with his wife. In one of our discussions, one of my clients talked about that void. He told me that he believed that more sex was the answer to filling the emptiness in his soul. That hallowed part of his soul could only be filled by God's Spirit. The solution is a solid identity in Christ. On the horizontal plane, the answer lies in authentic spousal intimacy.

Husbands, as wives, are divinely created with the need for a holistic love relationship. A marital relationship that incorporates commitment, friendship, and affection is highly likely to have a gratifying sexual life. Husbands need a spiritual and soul connection with their wives to have a gratifying sexual experience. Adam and Eve complemented each other in all three realms of the human experience. Adam became "joined to his wife," and the two were "united into one" (Gen. 2:24, NLT). This union included knowing (*yada*) each other in the realms of body, soul, and spirit.

Pleasing Him

Authentic sexual fulfillment for husbands, as wives, is a multi-dimensional engagement of spirit (commitment and sacrifice), soul (friendship), and body. It might take peeling back layers of a husband's heart in honest conversation to reveal his desire for a holistic sexual engagement. I have been privileged to listen to the longings of many husbands who wanted a greater emotional connection with their wives. After meeting with their husbands, this revelation was a pleasant surprise and, at times, unbelievable disclosure to some wives when discussed in a follow-up session.

Husbands' desire for sexual frequency is not solely for pleasure but also to find increased emotional intimacy with their wives, to connect heart to heart. Some husbands want to be closer to their wives but have never articulated it until they come into counseling. A wife honors her husband when her love demonstrates an understanding that his sexual need is multidimensional. The apostle Paul exhorts mature women in the Body of Christ to "urge the younger women to love their husbands" (Titus 2:4). This love includes the arena of sexuality incorporating physical, emotional, and spiritual components.

Both husbands and wives desire physical, spiritual, and emotional fulfillment in their sexual life. However, husbands typically have a greater need (frequency) for sexual pleasure than their wives. Conversely, wives generally have a greater need for an emotional connection with their husbands to experience sexual satisfaction.

Pleasuring Him

Creating a romantic ambiance in the bedroom enhances the joy and pleasure of sexual intimacy. It is well known that men are more easily aroused sexually by visual images regarding sex than women. King Solomon's wife attests to the truth, saying:

"I was a virgin, like a wall; now, my breasts are like towers. When my lover looks at me, he is delighted with what he sees" (Song 8:10, NLT).

Solomon himself elaborates on the physical attraction of his wife with exhilaration:

> How beautiful are your feet in sandals
> O prince's daughter!
> The curves of your hips are like jewels,
> The work of the hands of an artist...
> How beautiful and how delightful you are
> My love, with all your delights!
> Your stature is like that of a palm tree
> and your breasts like its clusters of dates.
> I said, "I will climb the palm tree;
> I will grasp its branches.
> Let your breasts be like clusters of the grapevine,
> And the fragrance of your breath like apples,
> And your kisses like the best wine!
> (Song 7:1, 6–9, Amp).

There are entire industries that capitalize on men's natural disposition to sexual arousal through visual stimuli. Such sectors include clothing design that produces provocative "creative fabrics" for women. A wife can be ingenious and alluring in dress, visually stimulating her husband in the bedroom.

Most husbands are also sexually incited by their spouse's perfume. King Solomon reveals his delight and compliments his wife on the superb choice of fragrance:

> How delightful is your love, my sister, my bride!
> How much more pleasing is your love than wine
> and the fragrance of your perfume more than any

> spice! Your lips drop sweetness as the honeycomb,
> my bride; milk and honey are under your tongue.
> The fragrance of your garments is like the fragrance
> of Lebanon (Song 4:10–11).

His Sexual Frequency

The topic of sexual frequency is one of the most common issues regarding sex for husbands in counseling. Wives often complain about the lack of love and affection, while husbands' focus is on sexual frequency. Most husbands are not transparent in counseling about this subject. However, they sometimes use subtle humor to make their point known. The following are two examples.

A husband, Charles (not his real name), accentuated his situation during a discussion on sex. The topic emerged from the "Prepare-Enrich" marriage assessment inventory that the couple completed. While glancing at his wife, Charles softly said, "Doc, you know I am a married man. Last week I read in the Proverbs that a married man should always be intoxicated with his wife's lovemaking. Thanks to Joyce (not the wife's real name), I am sober six days a week." Joyce chuckled in amusement. He referred to Proverbs 5:19, which tells a husband to let his wife's breasts satisfy him and always be intoxicated with her love.

Jose and Florence (not their real names) came in about some issues on cultural differences. They had been married just over one year. In the course of counseling, the subject of sex emerged. The discussions veered towards 1 Corinthians 7:5. This verse encourages married couples to meet sexual needs by engaging in sex frequently. The verse further elaborates that this gift to each other would avoid temptation from Satan. Jose contributed to the conversation by saying this in summary: "Our sex life is pretty good, but there is room for improvement. This marriage is till death do us part. Satan is not going to upset our marriage. I need more protection for Florence. We have sex twice a week, but I think we should increase that number to three to add an extra layer of protection from the evil one."

He said it in good spirits. We all laughed. Florence essentially nodded, as if to say, point taken.

In the "Prepare-Enrich" marriage assessment, there is a question on sex: "How often would you prefer or expect sex?" In a hundred-plus couples I assessed or verbally asked the question, husbands responded or recorded weekly numbers above their wives. In about half the cases, husbands' numbers were twice their wives'. I can only recall three instances where a wife's number was above her husband's.

A husband's frequency for sexual relations is God-given and a need that is important to him. Paul and Pauline (not their real names), who were in their late thirties, came in for counseling presenting conflict issues. They were both corporate professionals with two early elementary school-age children. Their schedule was hectic. The issue of sex emerged in the first few weeks of counseling. Paul complained that Pauline's job and tiredness resulted in very infrequent sex life and that he was angry about that. His anger was visible. Pauline admitted that she did not have the energy for sex.

I introduced an analogy comparing sex and Pauline's snack she took in her mid-morning break. They both got the meaning immediately, even before I spoke the second sentence. After the discussion, the couple decided to have a romantic sexual adventure on weekends compared to a full-course meal. They also agreed to snack once a week, with Pauline adding, "I know my husband, and I am a very creative woman."

Within a month, they had a good report that all was fine in their sex life. Consequently, Paul relaxed in sessions. Pauline disclosed that Paul was helping more with the housework and the children at home, even though she did not ask him. She felt less tired and more loved. We continued to work on their conflict issues but in a more amenable manner. Yes, sexual satisfaction can be a game-changer and a mood changer. Studies have found that sexual fulfillment can produce positive emotional changes in both husbands and wives.

His Frequency Sweet Spot

In gratitude for my suggestion on frequency to the couple, Paul, at the end of a session, exclaimed, "Dr. Wilson, I love you." Pauline was alarmed, and the expression on her face read: "Paul, I did not know this meant so much to you!" I also noticed that Pauline's language changed gradually. The first time she reported on counseling progress, among other things, she said, "I gave him a snack," her affect reflecting the joy of giving. Two months later, I inquired how the overall relationship was progressing. Pauline noted in the feedback: "We had two snacks last week," she smiled, with "we" implying mutual joy and pleasure. They both agreed that she was content, and Paul's frequency sweet spot was three times a week.

Sexual Oneness

Couples find sexual fulfillment when sex goes beyond physical pleasure to the joy and contentment of spirit and soul. The result is greater unity and security in the marriage. In such bonding experiences, the Spirit of God advances the ever-unveiling mystery of oneness.

I previously mentioned the following research studies that applied to wives. It is worth repeating here, for it is pertinent to both spouses and further emphasizes their significance. Several studies have reported that increased sexual satisfaction is linked positively with better moods, job satisfaction, and greater work production. Research has also found a circular effect between sex and genuine verbal and physical affection. When husbands selflessly share more love and affection, wives become more amorous, increasing sexual engagement. When wives are amenable to more frequency in sexual activity, husbands tend to become more helpful and affectionate. This cycle generally leads to spouses sharing warm, positive regard toward each other generating greater emotional intimacy. This sequence strengthens friendship and commitment toward maturing marital oneness.

Chapter 11

The Synergy in Covenant Marriage
To Form a More Perfect Union

God's Portrait of Love

First Corinthians 13 exemplifies God's portrait of love. The apostle Paul begins speaking about the language of humans and of angels and then pivots to the language of love declaring it as the most excellent way:

> What if I speak all languages of humans and of angels? If I did not love others, I would be nothing more than a noisy gong or a clanging cymbal…Love is patient; love is kind. It does not envy; it does not boast; it is not proud. It does not dishonor others, it is not self-seeking, it is not easily angered, and it keeps no record of wrongs. Love does not delight in evil but rejoices with the truth. It always protects, always trusts, always hopes, and always perseveres. (1 Cor. 13:1, 4–7, CEV)

The apostle Paul discussed unity and diversity of the Church concerning spiritual gifts in first Corinthians chapter 12. He compares the superiority of love over the spiritual gift of speaking in unknown languages. Paul continues with an in-depth description of the language of love in chapter 13, listing its many attributes.

These supernatural attributes define love. Every spouse desires their partner to live out these qualities, to be carriers of God's glory (Matt. 5:16). These attributes include patience, kindness, contentment, humility, gentleness, long-suffering, generosity, faithfulness, protectiveness, trust, and perseverance (1 Cor.13:4–7). When we live a life of submission to God, these virtues become home in our character (Deut.30:6). The Holy Spirit transforms us into the character image of Christ with ever-increasing likeness (2 Cor. 3:18).

God personifies the attributes of love, for God is love (1 Jn. 4:16). Love embodies the fruit of the Spirit through which married couples can authentically express love to each other. The Holy Spirit empowers spouses to love each other, to exemplify Jesus's love for the Church (Rom. 6:13). Jesus loves through us by the indwelling of the Holy Spirit (Gal. 2:20).

A Deed without Love is Dead

Previously we asserted that giving is the substance of love. However, one can deliver acts of "love" without possessing the attributes of love. It is a form without intimacy. Such actions are sometimes well-intentioned but intellectual and generated by covert self-centered motives. Unless these acts are expressions of the fruit of the Spirit, they are at best a resounding gong or a clanging cymbal (1 Cor. 13:1). The apostle Paul elucidates this in his letter to the Corinthian Church, stating:

> What if I speak all languages of humans and of angels? If I did not love others, I would be nothing more than a noisy gong or a clanging cymbal... What if I gave away all that I owned and let myself

be burned alive? I would gain nothing unless I loved others. (1 Cor. 13:1,3, CEV)

The passage above details giving all of one's possession to the poor, which resembles sacrificial love. But the apostle Paul says these acts without love mean nothing. These actions without love are performance-oriented, not originating from a spirit-filled heart. The doer does not exhibit the intrinsic attributes of love imparted by the Holy Spirit. A spouse can only express authentic love if God's law is written on their heart. Love written on our heart becomes our intrinsic nature, God in us (Col. 1:27). We, therefore, express God's nature (2 Pet. 1:4). If we do not choose to submit to Jesus Christ as Lord, we will operate with impure motives of "our old self" (Rom. 6:6).

The Lord Jesus called out the Pharisees for their overt actions that mimic genuine love. The Pharisees gave lip service to God without being the attributes of love:

"These people honor me with their lips, but their hearts are far from me. They worship me in vain; their teachings are merely human rules" (Matt. 15:8–9).

Love as the Essence of Your Being

Love essentially is not simply one's "good deeds," as the apostle Paul expounded to the Corinthians. Genuine acts of love emanate from God's divine nature. God has given every Christian a new heart that is "tender" and "responsive" to His love (Jerimiah36:26, NLT). When we are submitted to God's will, we reflect His love. Jesus is the personification of perfect love. The state of "being love" reflects the heart of God. God's love is "being" the fruit of the Spirit (such as being patient, being kind). God has shared His divine nature with you (2 Pet. 1:4). Thus, love is Christ in you expressing His life through you (Gal. 2:20). The product of such divine love is authentic deeds. Genuine acts of love emanate from the attributes that define love (1 Cor. 13).

The following narrative illustrates this concept of love as being and practice. Pastor Tony and First Lady Sheila (not their real names) came in for marriage counseling. Tony was a faithful and hardworking husband. Sheila was a devoted wife who worked at home with her three children. She also worked part-time as a real estate lawyer.

Pastor Tony and Sheila were an unhappy couple. Tony claimed that he did everything to make Sheila happy. Tony reported buying Sheila flowers and giving her cards and gifts. He occasionally brought her breakfast in bed and helped at home. They spent generously on hotels and restaurants. Tony sometimes complimented Sheila.

Sheila reported that Tony said hurtful words when she did not immediately meet his requests. Tony also revived old stories early in the marriage that placed Sheila in an unfavorable light. He frequently rebuked her. Sheila was scared of his anger and harsh criticism of any error she made. She seemed tense in the relationship.

The problem was not Pastor Tony's lack of action toward Sheila. He performed lots of deeds. Shelia did not believe that her husband's character reflected the virtues of covenant love. Tony's interpersonal engagements with her were hurting her. There was much contradiction between Tony's deeds to Sheila and his behaviors in interacting with her. Pastor Tony was apparently performing acts of "love," not love as an expression of his being. The apostle James wrote:

> Out of the same mouth come praise and cursing. My
> brothers and sisters, this should not be. Can both
> fresh water and saltwater flow from the same spring?
> My brothers and sisters, can a fig tree bear olives or
> a grapevine bear figs? Neither can a salt spring pro-
> duce fresh water. (Jm. 3:10–13)

Shelia wanted to be loved by her husband through the nature of the HolySpirit. Pastor Tony focused on how he believed Sheila wished to be loved, which was good in itself, but his acts without Holy Spirit attributes were "a resounding gong." He was not demonstrating the virtues of patience, kindness, and gentleness. Sheila desired a patient, kind, gentle, and caring husband. Sheila's most profound need in the marriage was that Tony reflects the meaning of authentic love of first Corinthians thirteen. My evaluation was that Tony needed to repent and surrender his will to the Spirit that his behavior would reflect God's love. Then he would genuinely love Shelia through the fruit of the Spirit—love, joy, peace, forbearance, kindness, goodness, faithfulness, gentleness, and self-control (Gal. 5:22–23). His acts would then be meaningful and fulfilling to Sheila.

Jesus is the personification of perfect love (1 Jn. 4:16). We possess God's love, but our expressions of Him are at times imperfect. When a wife says to me, "My husband is a kind man," I understand that her husband is not solely doing kind deeds, but kindness is a character trait at the core of his being. When a husband says, "My wife is a gentle person," I perceive that he is saying that his wife does not simply perform gracious behavior but that gentleness is a virtue at the center of her being. A person's behavior typically emanates from the heart of their convictions (Prov. 23:7). Let us reiterate God's definition of love. Love is being the fruit of the Spirit (such as being patient or being kind), expressed in words and deeds. You can genuinely love your spouse when Christ lives His divine attributes in you (Gal. 2:20).

On Becoming a Loving Person

When our primary relationship orients with God, our attachment with our spouse is rooted and nurtured in love (Matt. 6:33). On becoming a loving person, one is being transformed into the character of Christ. The more we surrender to the will and purposes of God, the more our marriage becomes an expression of love, who is Christ living in us the hope of marital joy and happiness (Col. 1:27). Then, and only then, are you enabled and impassioned to love your spouse as Christ loves the Church. We are confident that we can sincerely love our spouse as Christ loves the Church, for we know that we "participate in the divine nature" of Christ (2 Pet. 1:4).

God's Spirit awakens our soul and gives us the capacity to love genuinely. The apostle John encourages us to love one another and then proceeds to explain the source of that love and how to receive it:

> Dear friends, let us love one another, for love comes from God. Everyone who loves has been born of God and knows God. Whoever does not love does not know God because God is love. This is how God showed his love among us: He sent his one and only Son into the world that we might live through him (1 Jn. 4:7–8).

A loving person reflects God's glory through the indwelling of the Holy Spirit that manifests God's character (Jn. 15:8). A caring person wholeheartedly exudes "the fruit of the Spirit of love, joy, peace, forbearance, kindness, goodness, faithfulness, gentleness, and self-control" (Gal. 5:22–23). Love is made complete by demonstrating actions that emanate from the virtues inherent in your being. The apostle John encourages us, "Not merely say that we love each other; let us show the truth by our actions" (1 Jn. 3:18). Becoming a loving person enables us to love our spouse through loving submission to God. When "we love one another, God lives in us, and His love is brought to full expression in us" (1Jon 4:12, NLT).

Loving Your Spouse through Loving God

Understanding love begins with God, for God's very being is love (1 Jn. 4:7–8). God does not just possess love; He is love. Jesus was not just practicing the fruit of the Spirit. He was the personification of the fruit of the Spirit. Because God lives in us, "His love is made complete in us." We are then enabled to love one another (1 Jn. 4:12).

To abound in God's love, Jesus instructed us on his divine order of loving. Pursuing marriage oneness is first pursuing oneness with God. God is our first love (Matt. 22:36–40). Jesus also emphasized that love for God must exceed love for all, including the love for one's spouse (Lk. 14:26). Loving God and loving your spouse are mutually inclusive. You cannot optimally love your spouse without prioritizing your relationship with God. When you love your spouse, you love God, for "if we keep on loving others, we will stay one in our hearts with God, and he will stay one with us" (1 Jn 4:16, CEV).

God is the source of love and enables you to love your spouse. God establishes his love in our hearts. We become other-centered as we become conformed to the character of Christ (2 Cor. 3:18). The more you surrender to Christ, the greater your capacity to bear the fruit of the Spirit and become a great lover to your spouse (Gal. 2:20):

> Remain in me, as I also remain in you.
> No branch can bear fruit by itself; it must remain
> in the vine.
> Neither can you bear fruit unless you remain in me.
> I am the vine; you are the branches.
> If you remain in me and me in you,
> you will bear much fruit; apart from me, you can
> do nothing
> (Jn. 15:4–5).

The Symphony of Married Love: Loving Your Spouse Wholeheartedly

The symphony of marital love is weaving together sacrificial commitment (*ahava*), intimate friendship (*raya*), affection, and sexual intimacy (*dod*), producing the harmony of marriage oneness. The synergy of marital love is multifaceted incorporating spirit, soul, and body. Married partners fulfill spiritual, emotional, and physical needs by the gift of self as a continuous offering to each other. Jesus declared that you should love one another with your entire being, for married love is multidimensional (Matt. 22:37).

Loving your spouse in the holistic way described above requires partners to know each other intimately. Married lovers must understand their spouses' degree of preference for what brings them marital satisfaction. Your spouse is unique in what constitutes their needs and wants. The following analogy can be helpful. I take vitamin C, vitamin D, and zinc supplements to boost my immune system. My body needs each supplement in different amounts. I need the daily recommended 90 milligrams of vitamin C, but only 15 micrograms of vitamin D. Both are essential for good health.

Similarly, a wife may desire to date her husband every week but has less interest in receiving gifts at that frequency. She only looks forward to gifts four times a year: on their wedding anniversary, her birthday, Mother's Day, and Valentine's Day. She needs both romantic dates and gifts at different measures. However, together these two acts facilitate wholeness to their marital relationship. Not meeting these needs in their time and right measure may disturb the relationship.

Some couples may desire help in identifying their partner's love preferences. Dr. Gary Chapman, best-selling author, speaker, and marriage counselor, has developed an excellent resource. The "Love Language Quiz," available online, ranks five areas of preference a spouse desires to be loved. It helps in prioritizing your partner's love desires. A choice may score low, like vitamin D to the body but is no less essential for marital well-being in season.

For Christians loving is an art guided by the Holy Spirit in expressing holistic marital love. Loving your spouse with all your heart is to dance to the Song of all Songs. It is the sacred union of husband and wife with Christ as the head. This harmony of three is the bedrock of marriage oneness. It is the source of all true marital joy and passion and the cornerstone of marriage success. This seamless union of covenant love generates an unquenchable flame. The Song of Songs describes such love to be "as strong as death." *Ahava*, the fundamental concept of love as commitment and sacrifice, is used to represent the synergy of the three aspects of married love:

> Place me like a seal over your heart, like a seal on your arm; for love [*ahava*] is as strong as death, it's jealously unyielding as the grave. It burns like blazing fire, like a mighty flame. Many waters cannot quench love; rivers cannot sweep it away. If one were to give all the wealth of one's house for love, it would be utterly scorned (Song 8:6–7, parenthesis added).

The symphony of marital love is a dance that authenticates the fruit of the Spirit: joy, peace, kindness, patience, goodness, and faithfulness (Gal. 5:22–23, 1 Cor. 13:4–8). Lovers must be captivated by Jesus, the Bridegroom, to waltz gracefully to the Song of all Songs. It is a dance rhythm that only God's leading can perfect, for the Lord orders the steps (Ps. 37:23).

It is God, the Lover of your soul, who fulfills the spiritual needs of your spouse's heart. The love we give is Christ living through us, releasing His divine attributes in us (Gal. 2:20). God's holy character encapsulates joy, peace, patience, kindness, generosity, gentleness, and meekness. Married couples become expressers of God's divine nature, loving each other wholeheartedly in spirit, soul, and body by the gift of themselves. Covenant spouses are devoted to a life-time commitment, are faithful friends, and are passionate lovers. Covenant lovers glorify God by maintaining and progressively unveiling the sacred mystery of marriage oneness.

Part 3

Generative Oneness:

The Pathway of Marriage Longevity

Chapter 12

Homeland Security
The Biblical Model of the Christian Home

The Family Institution

This chapter explores the biblical ideal for the Christian home. The family is the first institution God established on earth. God's purpose for the family is to implement the principles of the family in Heaven. A healthy family is a secure and stable institution characterized by love, support, and a generative agenda.

The primary purpose of home and family is to let God's kingdom principles and precepts be represented on earth as it is Heaven (Matt. 6:10). God is the author of marriage and the ultimate arbiter on the organization and function of the family. God created the rules and principles that inform and govern marriage and family life. God's instructions on order and responsibility in the family ensure love, unity, and peace.

The Christian family is the nucleus of the kingdom of God on earth. Its culture, principles, and precepts represent the love and unity of the heavenly kingdom. The decline of a nation begins with the deconstruction of the family unit. The strength of any society and country is the strength of its families. The Christian family is the foundation of a virtuous, healthy, and prosperous community and nation (Prov. 14:24).

The First Family

The Garden of Eden was the first home on earth, and Adam and Eve were its first family. Adam was the first leader of the home, and Eve was the first lady in that institution. The Lord put Adam "into the garden of Eden to dress it and keep it" (Gen. 2:15, KJV). The Hebrew word for "keep" is *shamar*, translated as exercising diligent care to guard, preserve, and protect. Adam had to protect his home from evil coming from the outside. He was also responsible for safeguarding his family by spiritually fortifying them to resist temptations that may emerge from within the organization. Eventually, Adam did not diligently guard the garden, and Satan introduced sin into the human race.

Guarding the Home

God called Adam and Eve to guard the home and transmit marriage and family values, principles, and structures to future generations (Deut. 4:9). Today, God's instructions for the Christian home are the same as those given to Adam and Eve in their first home. In this day and age, these commandments are even more crucial. The family home is under siege. Satan attacks the family from within and without, sometimes in very subtle ways that mirror the proverbial frog in boiling water.

The world ridicules God's plan for the family, and some Christian couples fall for the gimmick presented as progress. The world's culture comes into the Christian home through education, entertainment, government, and the media. Parents are charged with the sacred responsibility to protect the family from the evil that may come from these media to influence the family's destiny.

Financial Responsibility

Guarding your home also means pursuing financial security and practicing financial responsibility. This book does not discuss this vital topic due to its scope and level of expertise needed to deliver excellence in this field. This subject would be more adequately addressed and more productive to couples when offered in a seminar/workshop format. There are excellent programs available in person or online. Many of these programs, such as Crown Financial, Barnabas Financial, and Financial Peace University, are offered in many churches.

Godly Offspring

God instituted a family system that seeks to protect children and provide for their healthy growth and development. Satan knows God's purpose for the family, which he violently opposes. The enemy seeks to obstruct God's plan that Christians have godly offspring. He has flooded the world with every evil imaginable. Christians need to be vigilant guards over their homes against worldly philosophies that threaten to dismantle the Judeo-Christian family foundation. God desires that biblical moral and ethical values transfer to future generations:

"Has not the one God made you? You belong to him in body and spirit. And what does the one God seek? Godly offspring. So be on your guard..." (Mal. 2:15).

God's Word reminds us not to be ignorant of the enemy's devices lest he outwits us and take advantage of us (2 Cor. 2:11). Satan's schemes are not always to cause sins of commission but also sins of omission. That is failure to follow God's commands. One of the most common errors in marriage and family life is ignoring explicit biblical principles for marital success. This omission is usually due to adopting the world's culture of individualism rather than seeking God's good, pleasing, and perfect will of cooperation and submission (Rom. 12:1–2).

I have counseled a millennial couple who were unaware that God had a divine design for marriage and family. They shared their plans to have a baby, and in their preparations, they included arrangements to take care of the child three weeks after the mom returned to work. The truth about God's design for the family was not in their consciousness. These young people were reacting to the contemporary culture. This moment seemed to be the first time they realized that God had instructions for family functioning. I cited this example because the couple admitted being financially secure and that the wife said that she was only working for "personal fulfillment." Her definition of personal fulfillment was working in the marketplace with her peers. She admitted that she never considered motherhood in light of God's plan for her life or as bringing fulfillment. Unlike many couples whose only other option is radical faith, they had choices.

Fathers and mothers are responsible for preserving the values of the Judeo-Christian family. The main job in a Christian home is to establish and preserve the kingdom principles and values of marriage and family. The Christian family is entrusted with transmitting godly heritage to each generation. Fathers are principally responsible for leading in the parental role (Prov. 1:8–9, 23:22,24, Eph. 6:4, 1 Tim. 3:4–5). A husband and wife in a loving and stable relationship facilitate godly parenting. Godly parenting can transform society (Matt. 5:13).

Family Modeled after the Heavenly Pattern

Adam and Eve sinned in the Garden of Eden. Thereon humanity possessed a fallen nature. God instituted his plan of salvation. He killed an animal and covered Adam and Eve with the skin representing His righteousness. The blood of the animal was a symbolic substitute that covered their sins. This sacrifice was a shadow until the Redeemer, the true Lamb of God, restored all things.

God also instituted a family model to ensure love, order, peace, and harmony. This marriage and family organizational and inter-actional structures are throughout God's Word. These models are the governmental expressions of the principles of the kingdom of God in Heaven (Matt. 6:10).

Marital Roles Scripturally Predetermined

The sacred order of marriage did not evolve over the ages. The marriage institution has a divine origin. God instituted male and female roles to keep marriage whole, ensuring stability and lon-gevity of the union. The path to success in marriage is marked in advance so that married couples can walk intentionally (Eph. 2:10, Heb. 12:1). God desires that his kingdom truths reign supreme in married life. The Lord instituted roles for marital peace, joy, and prosperity. God assigned functions so that a husband and wife would complement and not compete with each other. God's plan is immutable. God's unchanging Word consistently meets the needs of an ever-changing world.

God placed an innate desire in both husband and wife to take care of each other according to their divinely assigned roles. When God designates a function, he provides the inherent propensity for the role. Many couples have indicated their desire to take care of their spouse in the manner prescribed in God's Word. These tender moments sometimes start a conversation on family roles and func-tions. Marital roles are God's foundational pathway for spouses to love each other according to the divine plan. God's design for the family creates stability in marriages. It is equally valid that God instituted this model to nurture the growth and development of godly offspring to guide future generations.

Husband: Keeper of the Garden

God commissioned Adam to *shamar* (keep) the home and family. As you recall, *shamar* is to exercise diligent care to guard, preserve, and protect. God delegated the family leadership role to Adam (Gen. 2:16). A covenant husband derives his right to lead from God. He assumes the position with the consent of his covenant wife, who affirms and supports his leadership. The apostle Paul states the order of headship in the nuclear household relating it to the order in the heavenly family:

"But I want you to realize that the head of every man is Christ, and the head of the woman is the man, and the head of Christ is God" (1 Cor.11:3).

A husband can lead more capably when he first satisfactorily functions to ensure economic security for the home and serves in the priesthood ministry for his family. I have found in hundreds of cases that the marital relationship improves significantly when these two offices become securely established. Above all, a husband can lead most effectively when he willingly submits to God. Then he can successfully pursue oneness in marriage to love his wife as Christ loves the Church.

God's first command to Adam was to keep the garden. Adam had to cultivate the land to meet his family's material needs. Tending the field was his vocation and God's plan for the Edenic family:

"Then the LORD God took the man and put him in the Garden of Eden to tend and keep it" (Gen. 2:15, emphasis added).

Today, the keeper of the Garden would involve employment in the myriads of economic opportunities in the marketplace, including entrepreneurial ventures. From this primary role, Adam could perform his other functions adequately. Husbands are given the principal roles of provider (Gen. 2:15, 3:17, 19), protector (1 Pet. 3:7, Eph. 5:28, 1 Pet. 3:7), and leader (Gen. 3:16, Eph. 5:23,25, 1 Tim. 3:4). We all seek value and purpose in life, whether we choose to be single or married. The covenant husband finds temporal and eternal significance in marriage by following God's model for marriage and family.

Wife: Keeper of the Home

God designated Eve as Adam's helper. They were equal partners with different functions. The Hebrew word for helper is *ezer kenegedo*, translated as a helper, like his opposite and complement. In the Book of Genesis, Eve's role is "a helper as a partner" (NRS) and "a helper comparable to him" (NKJV). The apostle Peter describes Eve's role as "an equal partner in God's gift of life" (1 Pet. 3:7 NLT).

The biblical meaning of "helper" does not have the same connotation as today's definition. Webster defines "helper" as a relatively unskilled worker assisting a skilled worker. God is called our "helper." This reference to God depicts a function, not a position (Ps. 118:7, Heb. 13:6). This analogy applies to marriage. Helper is not a hierarchical position but a function. For example, a wife may excel her husband in some areas, including leadership and organizational skills. But she still functions alongside him in her biblical role as helpmate and equal partner.

God commissioned Eve to *shamar* (keep) the home by exercising diligent care to guard, preserve, and protect the family. God's first command to Eve was to be the keeper of the Home. Eve's vocation was the management of the family home. A godly and capable wife diligently manages her household. The Word of God counsels wives:

"To be discreet, chaste, keepers at home, good, obedient to their own husbands that the word of God be not blasphemed" (Titus 2:5, KJV).

Paul's letter to Timothy reiterates this counsel when he asserts that wives should "manage their homes and give the enemy no opportunity to slander" (1 Tim. 5:14). The Old Covenant also concurs with Paul on the plan for the family (Prov. 14:1, 31:27).

The administration of the home and tending to family responsibilities have both temporal and eternal implications. The covenant wife manages her household (Prov. 31:7), serves as the primary family caregiver and nurturer (Prov. 31:15), and is the immediate early childhood educator (Titus 2:4–5). God has naturally endowed women with a nurturing nature to engender a warm and secure home environment.

The virtuous and capable wife also functions in leadership roles in endeavors that correlate with her education, training, skills, and gifting (Prov. 31:10–31). The home is where parents teach sacred values and where a virtuous and strong character develops. A wife is the co-conservator of family values and traditions.

Creating a stable home is the cradle of a healthy society and civilization itself. As I previously noted, we all seek value and purpose in life whether we choose to be single or married. The covenant wife will find temporal and eternal significance when following God's design for marriage and family.

Marriage Equality, Unity, and Interdependence

God's marital model for Adam and Eve and all humanity is one of equality, unity, and interdependence (1 Cor. 11:11). This pattern exemplifies the relationship of the Father, the Son, and the Holy Spirit (2 Cor. 13:14). The divine paradigm brings order and meaning to marriage. It provides a framework for decision-making of life issues and family interactions. It establishes a foundation for cooperation in achieving marital, family, and societal goals.

Covenant spouses work together to accomplish their mission and goals, which God prepared for their fulfillment and His glory (Eph. 2:10). Adam had the ultimate responsibility for the family's functioning. God created Adam and Eve with unique, innate gender attributes suitable for marriage and family functioning roles.

The biblical roles of a husband and wife are ordered to produce structure, relational harmony, and clarity of purpose. Both husband and wife are functional leaders in their respective roles in the home. Spouses also assist in secondary capacities with each other's responsibilities. This organizational structure and interactional pattern are God's ideal design for marriage and family.

The biblical model for marriage and family prepares husbands and wives to fulfill family roles scripturally predetermined to maximize marital joy and happiness. These marital models include family organizational structures, mores, and values.

Restoring the Ancient Landmarks

A landmark is an object in a landscape that serves as a guide in the direction of one's course. It is a structure used as a point of orientation in locating other structures. A landmark is a recognizable natural or artificial feature used for navigation that stands out in its immediate environment. The Word of God asserts we should not remove the ancient landmarks established by our ancestors (Prov. 22:28).

In the spiritual sense, biblical landmarks give direction and orient Christians to scriptural truths in navigating the path of a godly life. God's ancient landmarks are immovable, for God is the same today, yesterday, and forever, and His Word endures infinitely (Heb. 13:8, 1 Pet. 1:25). God has not moved His landmarks for marriage and the family. The principles, precepts, values, organizational structures, and interactional patterns are as relevant today as when God first imparted them (Ex. 3:14, Rev. 1:8).

The Family Diner

The family dinner is a landmark that has diminished in contemporary society. The family diner is not just a facility to meet and eat. It is the place that establishes the family structure and facilitates social and emotional growth and development. The family dinner table is where the family gathers at set times. It is a place where routinely scheduled meetings become pillars of security and stability for a husband, a wife, and children. The hub of family life revolves around the family diner.

The following story may help to illustrate the importance of the family diner. A family came for counseling at the Christian organization where I ministered. The issue was chaos in the family. The husband and wife, committed Christians, had been married for about nine months and had lost control of the family dynamics. They were a blended family with five boys and three girls ranging from ages five to sixteen. The wife was a homemaker. The size of my office necessitated standing room in the first session. Briefly, they needed structural family counseling and communication skills, beginning with the parents. Over five months, we utilized several strategies undergirded by foundational biblical principles.

What helped this family were basic communication strategies, weekly family devotion, and a biweekly family conference to address the issues. I also revealed to them that I, too, grew up in a nuclear family with ten members. That knowledge boosted their confidence. The family reported that the most helpful intervention was the structured family scheduled meals at a set time around two joined tables. One mealtime rule was to encourage and celebrate the success of family members however minute. Serious issues were reserved for the family conference. This family gathering happened at least once a day with all family members present. Previously they had no set time, and they ate in small, segregated groups, basically by the family of origin.

The structural guidance provided brought order in the home and increased social interaction. The family understood each other better in the new setting under relatively pleasant conditions. The husband's leadership was taxed, but he prevailed well. The wife became very innovative in what can be described as a most challenging managerial task. Over time, both husband and wife reported more harmony, security, and intimacy in their marriage, greatly crediting the role of the family diner.

The Family Sanctuary

Restoring the ancient landmarks of marriage and family begin with making the home a family sanctuary. Dr. John Garr, Ph.D., in his book *Family Sanctuary: Restoring the Biblically Hebraic Home*, writes:

> Each home must view itself as a sanctuary, a mini-temple in which all the functions of biblical community life have their beginnings and are fully manifest. Doing so will restore a God-consciousness to both the church and society that will transcend the nominal Christian or Jewish experience. It will return the family of God to a face-to-face relationship of walking with God. It will be Eden renewed in the family sanctuary. (Garr 2003, 58)

The family sanctuary is the spiritual equivalent of the family dinner. All other family structures are rooted and grounded in the spiritual activities of the family sanctuary. Couples, with the husband's leadership, should establish an altar, a place with designated times for family devotions in their home. An altar is a place to meet with God.

Family devotions have enormous implications in fostering marital fulfillment and success. By devotions, I mean a time of relational engagement with God and family in the family sanctuary. Family devotions would include Bible reading, prayer, family blessings, and praise and worship. The priority in founding a Christian home is establishing an altar with appointed times to meet regularly with the Divine Head of the marriage. I believe that pastors, priests, and rabbis can play a transformational role in marshaling the husbands in their congregations to activate the priesthood in their homes. In the absence of a husband, a single head of household should lead in the family devotions.

Making Your Home a House of God

The family institution is the domestic church where love, care, faith, hope, prayer, forgiveness, commitment, respect, and sacrifice find a home. It is the place where true identity in Christ forms and develops.

It is not within the scope of this book to explore the rich concepts of the family sanctuary. I strongly recommend Dr. John D. Garr's book *Family Worship: Making Your Home a House of God.* It is a great family resource. It is a Christ-centered model in making your home a family sanctuary that adheres to Judeo-Christian values.

Generative Oneness

God thinks trans-generationally. For example, God speaks to Israel about their deliverance from captivity when fulfillment occurs in their descendants' time, many generations thereafter (Jer. 29:14, Ezek. 36:24).

God's heart is that Christians leave a legacy to the next generation. Most Christians think of leaving a material legacy. Such bequests are usually given by providing children with education or skills and material possessions. As much as it is essential to leave an inheritance to the next generation to make a living, it is equally important to impart a heritage of virtuous living. God's top priority is a spiritual legacy. It is a legacy of God's ways through instruction and example. God's purpose is to relay his precepts to each succeeding generation, to our "children and their children after them" (Deut. 4:9).

Deviation from God's manual on marriage in one generation creates a breach in the generational transmission of His blessings. The marital statistics of Christian marriages today, compared to previous generations, sound an evident alarm that the wall has been breached. God seeks godly offspring from his people from generation to generation (Mal. 2:15). He promises blessings for a thousand generations to those who keep his commandments (Deut. 7:9).

The family home is the foundational institution of society. God has given us a manual with instructions and principles that imitates the pattern of God's love for his bride, the Church. God has given us his Spirit to empower our walk to pursue marital oneness. Married couples who follow God's purpose for marriage fulfill his unique plan for their lives as one (Rom. 12:2). Living out God's will in marriage is to paint a portrait of the love of Christ and the Church. This lifestyle engenders blessings to todays' and future generations' natural and spiritual offspring.

Chapter 13

The Ministry of the Covenant Husband
Leadership to Provide, Protect, and Serve

A Holy Calling

*T*his chapter is the longest one in this book. That implies the tremendous leadership responsibilities of a husband and a father. The most in-depth instructions on marriage in the Bible is Ephesians chapter 5, verses 22–33. God devotes twice as many verses to the husband; the husband's role incorporates eight verses and the wife four. The ministry of the covenant husband is God's plan for the role of a husband in the Christian family. This chapter describes God's model for marriage from the husband's perspective.

This chapter outlines the covenant husband's roles and responsibilities in marital ministry. Covenant marriage is a hallowed institution with the divine headship of Jesus Christ. A Christian man who enters marriage has the sacred duty of representing the love of Christ to the Church. It should be the goal of every Christian husband to bring glory to God by fulfilling the biblical mandate of the covenant husband.

Marriage launches a man into a covenant relationship with his wife and God into marriage and family ministry. Marriage is answering the holy call from God to embark on family ministry submitted under the loving authority of Christ Jesus as King and as High Priest (1 Cor.11:3, Rom. 8:34).

God did not leave the role of the husband to an experiential process. When a person enters employment with an organization, there is a written job description. Likewise, God penned a job description for the vocation of a husband. He also defines the role of the father for the husband who assumes that position. God's divine power has given husbands all that is needed to find success in marriage and family life (2 Pet. 1:3).

The sacred orders for marriage ministry come from God, who officiated the first wedding and wrote the manual for marriage success. This manual has structural and interactional features for harmonious functioning in marriage. The husband's role is custom-designed to produce love and security for his wife and glory to God.

The Divine Headship of Marriage

Marriage is a sacred calling and ministry for those who choose to enter. The husband is the family priest/pastor/rabbi leading and serving his household under the headship of Jesus Christ and in the power of the Holy Spirit (Gal. 2:20). The marriage leadership structure is not of earthly origin. It is a divine order of headship. The head of Christ is God, the head of the husband is Christ, and the head of the wife is the husband (1 Cor.11:3). The husband's leadership operates not in perfection but is a daily progression toward greater unity with his wife (Prov. 4:18). The covenant husband does not live by fiat but by modeling the virtues of Christ, the exemplary Bridegroom.

Role of the Husband: Pathways in Loving Your Wife

Successful marriages are the outcome of spiritual ways and means. God instituted the husband's role as the primary way to love his wife. The husband's role is God's fundamental way for him to take care of his wife. God's instructions on spouses' role in marriage should be the most important question for couples, whether they are planning to get married or they have already married. The primary role of the covenant husband in marriage is to provide caring and responsible leadership for the family and love his wife as Christ loves the Church. As already mentioned, the biblical functions assigned to the husband are leader (Gen. 3:16, Eph. 5:22–24, 1 Cor. 11:3, Col. 3:18, 1 Pet. 3:1–6), provider (Gen. 2:15, 3; 17, 19), and protector (1 Pet. 3:7, Eph. 5:28). As you remember, the Hebrew word *ahava* defines sacrifice and commitment. The root word of *ahava* is *ahav*, which means to give, nurture, be devoted to another, and provide and protect what is given as a privileged gift. Love, therefore, epitomizes the role of the husband. To be an effective leader in marriage, a husband must first be a devoted follower of Christ manifesting His love.

Fatherhood

One of Satan's primary purposes is to influence the family by promoting father absence. By father absence, I mean a single-mother home. But I am also referring to homes with fathers who are not involved in their children's lives. The empirical research is overwhelming regarding the possible adverse effects of father absence and what has been termed "father hunger" in children and some adults. The redemptive news is that by the grace of God, some women have raised balanced and emotionally and socially healthy citizens through the love of the heavenly Father.

Fathers significantly affect their children's destinies. There are excellent resources to assist fathers who desire to be Father of the Year to their children. A good source is The National Center for Fathering resource center online. Online father education can increase fathers' involvement with their children. My doctoral dissertation on "The Effects of Web-based Parenting Education on Father Involvement" found a statistically significant increase in fathers' involvement with their children after participating in an online parenting program (Wilson, 2003).

The study also reported behavioral changes of practical significance following the web-based fathering interventions. These results were from eighty-nine fathers participating in a program that involved structured readings of articles and blogs online from two websites; *The National Center for Fathering* and *FatherWorks*. The sample included 67 percent African American fathers. Godly fathering is beneficial for both child development and marital harmony

Leadership That Serves Her

Adam was assigned the leadership role in the first marriage (Gen. 3:16). Later, the husband's position is affirmed in the New Covenant (Eph. 5:22–24). What does leadership in marriage look like? Our Lord Jesus answers the question in Matthew's gospel. The mother of James and John asked Jesus whether her two sons could sit on his right and left hand when he came into the kingdom. The other ten apostles got wind of it and became indignant. Jesus called them together and said:

> Ye know that the princes of the Gentiles exercise dominion over them, and they that are great exercise authority upon them. But it shall not be so among you: but whosoever will be great among

you, let him be your minister, and whosoever will
be chief among you, let him be your servant: Even as
the Son of man came not to be ministered unto, but
to minister, and to give his life a ransom for many.
(Matt. 20:25–28, KJV).

Let us examine the key points in Jesus's teaching to his apostles.
First, Jesus states what authentic leadership is not. He mentions
that the leaders in the world lord it over their people and flaunt
their authority. Jesus then goes on to explain that genuine leadership is service.

Jesus clarified that he came to earth to serve and not be served.
He exemplified servant leadership when he washed the apostles'
feet, which was the normal duty of a servant in Israel (Jn. 13:1–17).
Jesus's ultimate act of service is the sacrifice of himself for his bride,
the Church. Therefore, a husband's leadership should imitate Christ
by modeling humble acts of kindness and humility to his wife in
sacrificially ministering to her needs.

Leadership as Family Provider

In the beginning, God told Adam that one of his roles in marriage was the keeper of the Garden (Gen. 2:15). Adam's chief role
was to cultivate the field in providing for his family. After the fall,
Adam was reminded of his responsibility to dress the Garden. But
this time with much greater toil (Gen. 3:17–19). Adam's role was
one of the primary ways to be a servant leader to Eve.

The fundamental mandate to the husband is the responsibility
to provide for the maintenance of the home and meet his family's
needs. This is exemplified in the historical Hebrew culture. After
a man proposes to marry a woman, he immediately goes away to
build a house with all the amenities for his bride. Jesus illustrated

this in a parable describing his preparation and returns for his bride the Church (Jn. 14:23).

While the bridegroom is building the house, the bride prepares to build a home modeled after the pattern described in Proverbs 31. Her preparation includes resources to establish a godly family. The general conclusion indicates that the husband builds the house as the provider, and the wife secures the home as manager and nurturer. The home is the human resource center and social and spiritual hub for healthy and generative family life.

Scripturally, husbands are the primary income producer, but wives sometimes generate supplemental income (Prov. 310). Although a wife is the direct family caregiver and home manager, husbands support their wives in their responsibilities. Both spouses assist each other in their respective roles. All marital obligations have primary and support functions. However, it is scripturally clear that a husband is the primary provider and executive leader, and a wife is the homemaker and primary nurturer. Both are equal in God's heavenly gift of life and equal partners in possession of all earthly resources (1 Pet. 3:7).

Leadership That Protects Her

An essential responsibility for the covenant husband is to protect and serve his wife and household (1 Tim. 3:12). The protection of one's wife, as we discussed earlier, is a sacred trust given by God to a husband. As you would remember, the foundational Hebrew word for love is *ahava*, which is commitment and sacrificial love. The essence of *ahava* love is to be devoted to another to provide and protect.

The husband's duty to protect is an element of God's definition of love. "Love always protects, always trusts, always hopes, and always perseveres" (1 Cor. 13:7). A husband's leadership responsibilities to protect include accountability for whatever happens in the home. This precedent was set in the Garden of Eden when Adam and Eve sinned. When God came looking for someone to be ultimately accountable and take responsibility, he called for Adam, the head of the family.

The Song of Songs illustrates the husband's devotion to protecting his wife. The bride compares Solomon's protection to the covering of a banner (Song 2:4). The banner over the bride signifies affection and security.

The apostle Paul affirms the responsibility of a husband to protect and care for his wife. This protection incorporates physical and financial security. It also implies social and emotional safeguards. The apostle Paul reminds husbands to "love your wives and do not be harsh with them" (Col. 3:19). The apostle Peter also gives an excellent explanation on how a husband should protect his wife's emotional well-being:

> In a similar way, you husbands must live with your wives in an understanding manner, as with a most delicate partner. Honor them as heirs with you of the gracious gift of life so that nothing may interfere with your prayers (1 Pet. 3:7, ISV).

One of my clients related her experience of her husband's emotional protection. We were discussing their strengths from their Prepare Enrich marriage assessment inventory results. I incorporate couples' areas of strength in finding resolutions. She related that her husband protected her feelings regardless of the situation, whether they differed in opinion or the offense was hers. She said that he chooses his words carefully and is always encouraging. It was one of their memorable moments.

Leadership That Respects Her

First, let us establish the meaning of respect in covenant marriage to enhance our understanding of its application. Let us say what respect is not. Respect is not stroking the ego. That is vain pride. The Merriam-Webster Dictionary defines respect as: "expressions of high or special regard; to consider worthy of high regard; an act of giving particular attention; to recognize the worth of a person."

A husband must lead by emulating Christ's love in honoring his wife. Authentic leadership in marriage is a relationship characterized by warmth, care, and respect. Husbands must love their wives as Christ loved the Church (Eph. 5:25). Husbands should be considerate as they live with their wives and "treat them with respect" as equal partners so that nothing will hinder their prayers (1 Pet. 3:7). God has placed great value on a husband honoring his wife's need for respect such that his prayers are hindered for not doing so!

A husband's genuine respect for his wife indicates his love for her. A husband cannot fully love his wife without respecting her, for "love is patient, and kind. Love is not jealous or boastful or proud or rude" (1 Cor. 13:4–5, NLT). Love embodies respect. To respect her is to love her. Respect is a universal human need. It is sometimes more critical to some individuals due to cultural upbringing.

A wife's need for respect is as crucial as her husband's. A husband's need for respect in marriage is generally more associated with his wife's perception and responses to his work, leadership, and authority in the home (Eph. 5:22–24). A wife's desire for respect is generally more aligned with her sense of worth relating to her family role and her husband's love and confidence in her (Prov. 31:10–11, 28).

Mutual Respect

The Word of God underscores the importance of mutual respect between spouses for an equally honoring relationship. The Word counsels the covenant wife to" respect her husband" (Eph.5:33). The Lord reminds husbands that a wife "is worth far more than rubies," which implies deep respect, signifying high regard for her person-hood (Prov.31:10).

Respect is a universal human need for both genders, as revealed in Scripture and confirmed in my counseling experience. A husband typically displays hurt and anger over overt disrespect or lack of respect from his wife. A wife typically responds to disrespect with feelings of pain and resentment. I have had more wives complain of lack of respect from their husbands than men have about their wives. I am also aware that husbands are generally hesitant to speak in counseling and less about respect from their wives. Disrespect is a human issue with different gender and cultural responses to its expression.

Respect implies the care and worth one attaches to a spouse in the marital relationship (Prov. 31:10). When spouses respect each other, there is an evolving strength and confidence in their marital union. Mutual and equal respect is a biblical precept and essential for husbands and wives. Respect is at the core of marital oneness (1 Pet. 3:7, Eph. 5:33).

The song "Respect," written and recorded by Otis Redding (a husband), and later widely popularized by singer Aretha Franklin (a wife), underscores both a husband's and a wife's soul need for respect as an expression of love. The Aretha version touched a chord in women and became a hit that galvanized women's movements nationwide into social activism.

The covenant husband who truly respects his wife will find that "she is worth far more than rubies" (Prov. 31:10). Healthy self-worth is rooted in our identity with Christ. A strong identity in

Christ generates secure self-worth and facilitates a healthy emotional attachment in marriage (2 Cor. 5:17, 1 Pet. 2:9). Our identity in Christ is to believe and live in the value of what God says we are. For example, God says that we are loved (Jn. 3:16), we are his masterpiece (Eph. 2:10), a royal priesthood (1 Pet. 2:9), and a new creation (2 Cor. 5:17). We identify as God's family, sons and daughters of our Father in Heaven (2 Cor. 6:18).

Leadership in Family Decision-Making

One of the husband's critical areas of leadership in marriage is decision-making for his family. Because of his assigned role as head of the home, the covenant husband is the final decision maker of the family while always yielding to Jesus Christ (through His Word), the ultimate authority of the marriage union. A husband takes responsibility for the results of decisions made in his family, even when he delegates the final decision to his wife on any family issue (Gen. 3:8–11, Josh. 24:15). Biblical principles guide the covenant husband to execute the functions of his office as the head of his family.

A husband should live by the truth that God is the source of all revelation for wise decision-making. The Holy Spirit is the all-wise Counselor that will guide a husband and a wife into all truth (Jn. 16:13). Married couples should prayerfully seek wisdom and understanding for decision-making from God, "who gives generously to all" (Jm. 1:5). The Lord will answer those who seek him (Ps. 34:4). Search the Word of God for a biblical principle or precept that undergirds the issue in making any decision. The Word has all the wisdom we need for this life (2 Pet. 1:3).

Joint Decision Making

Wise couples realize that the very nature of oneness in marriage warrants joint decision-making (Eccl. 4:9). A husband should be mindful that his wife is his complement in the marriage union. A wife comes to the marriage with gifting, skills, education, and unique experiences that enrich the marriage. The wife may possess specific knowledge and expertise that exceed the husband's capabilities in some areas. The wise husband incorporates the treasures of his wife's life experiences and affirms her contribution to decision-making on all major family issues (Prov. 11:14).

The honorable husband does not micromanage his wife's operation in administering her family responsibilities. His leadership in decision-making relates to significant issues that will affect the overall process and direction of the marital union and the family as a unit. As the covenant husband considers the needs of the family, he sacrificially puts the desires of his wife above his own (Phil. 2:3). Such sacrifices (to draw near) enhance marital intimacy.

The capable and virtuous wife of Proverbs 31 is the scriptural model of the function and role of the godly wife. The capable wife functions with autonomy and executes her business ventures in the home and the marketplace. Proverbs 31 implies that the capable wife consults with her husband in making significant decisions. However, the final decision is hers. She also has autonomy in her expertise regarding her personal life decisions and entrepreneurial undertakings. For example, she makes significant decisions with her earnings when "she evaluates a field and buys it" and then proceeds to plant a vineyard (Prov. 31:16). She then shares her profits with the poor (Prov. 31:20).

Spiritual Leadership

Spiritual leadership is fundamental in having a healthy Christian family life. The husband is the priest/pastor/rabbi of the family home. The principal institution for spiritual education is the home under the leadership of the husband and father. The husband and father should ensure that the home is the central place for spiritual instruction, with the Church being the enrichment center. All Christians are part of the priesthood of believers. God authorized the leadership in the Christian home to function in the role of a priest to the family:

"But you are a chosen people, a royal priesthood, a holy nation, God's special possession, that you may declare the praises of him who called you out of darkness into his wonderful light" (1 Pet. 2:9).

How important is it for a couple to engage in spiritual practices? It is the bedrock of the Christian home. When we become Christians, our dormant spirit awakes. The appetite for spiritual nourishment, once nonexistent, became alive, and the heart began to hunger and thirst after spiritual righteousness:

- "In the past, you were spiritually dead because of your disobedience and sins... that while we were spiritually dead in our disobedience, He brought us to life with Christ. It is by God's grace that you have been saved" (Eph. 2:1, 4–5, GNT).

- "You were at one time spiritually dead because of your sins and because you were Gentiles without the Law. But God has now brought you to life with Christ" (Col. 2:13, GNT).

The born-again Christian now has this new spiritual need. The spirit man is now awakened and needs spiritual nourishment from the Word of God (Matt. 4:4). God is the source of true love. In counseling, I sometimes ask couples to list the top five needs in their marriage. Most Christian wives include engaging in prayer and Bible study with their husbands.

Spiritual disciplines are the foundational cornerstone that gives purpose and direction in marriage. Marriage becomes more meaningful, and the marital journey takes on greater temporal and eternal significance. It becomes vital that husbands lead and facilitate the family's growth and development through spiritual activities. The Word of God charges husbands to lead in that responsibility (Eph.

5:25–26). Spiritual practices enhance our intimacy with Christ and promote life transformation.

Leadership in Couple Devotions

Couple devotion is fellowship with God for a more intimate relationship (Phil. 3:10). Meeting with God is being in His presence. Christian couples must engage in spiritual practices. God's presence, and our interaction with Him, stirs His divine love in us. His love generates the blessings that engender practical oneness. God's presence through couple devotions imparts God's living Word. In the Old Covenant, the Ark of God was the presence of God. When the Ark of the Covenant temporarily resided in the household of Obed-Edom, his family was abundantly blessed with God's presence:

"The ark of God remained with the family of Obed-Edom in his house for three months, and the LORD blessed his household and everything he had" (1 Chron.13:14).

Appointed Times

Couple devotion can be spontaneous but is best and more productive when scheduled. This pattern is in the Word. There were daily scheduled times for spiritual devotions (Acts 3:1). My wife Sherron and I meet four times a week for spiritual devotions. We reserve the rest of the days for meeting alone with the Lord to pursue a deeper and more personal relationship with Jesus. It is profitable when spouses commit such solitary time to meet in their secret place with Jesus (Ps. 91:1). Jesus frequently sought a private place to be with His Father, routinely, and in times of sorrow (Mark 1:35, Matt. 14:12–13). Each couple must schedule their own time that works best for them. In God's presence, married couples find faith and discover the ever-unveiling mystery of oneness.

Couple Bible study allows God to speak kingdom principles of oneness in guiding couples and to release the blessings of marriage. The Word of God is a lamp to our feet and a light on our path (Ps. 119:105). The Word is the cornerstone of the marital structure. Our Lord Jesus underscored the monumental significance of the Word when he declared that the fulfilled life is living by "every word that comes from the mouth of God" (Matt. 4:4). I suggest you start with a good devotional or read a book of the Bible.

Couple prayer is imperative for spiritual growth, intimacy with God, and emotional bonding in marriage. Prayer is a great way to get to know God and your spouse. Prayer is all about relationships. Speaking to Father God creates vulnerability and an opportunity to listen to Him and hear your spouse's heart. It is out of the heart that the mouth speaks (Lk. 6:45). It is in unity that God bestows his blessings on his children. When married couples are united in prayer, their victories can increase exponentially (Deut. 32:30):

> How good and pleasant it is when God's people live together in unity!
> It is like precious oil poured on the head running down on the beard, running down on Aaron's beard, down on the collar of his robe.
> It is as if the dew of Hermon were falling on Mount Zion.
> For there the Lord bestows his blessing, even life forevermore
> (Ps. 133:1–3).

Couple praise and worship should not be relegated to Saturday or Sunday Sabbath time at the church or temple. God seeks worshippers who "will worship the Father in spirit and in truth" (Jn. 4:23). The home is as a mini-church. The original Christian churches met in homes. Later these home gatherings extended into community congregations (Acts1:3, 1 Cor. 16:19, Rom. 16:5).

Celebrating Sabbath with one's spouse facilitates marriage intimacy. I would suggest couples enter into the fullness of the biblical Sabbath celebration. By Sabbath, my focus here is not on a day, Saturday or Sunday, worship, but communion with God in rest and celebration. This sanctified day in His presence will enhance your relationship with the Lord and increase marital intimacy with your spouse.

Family blessings is one of the most important acts of a husband and father's leadership in the Christian home. Some of the patriarchs in the Hall of Faith are mentioned solely for their act of blessing:

"By faith, Isaac blessed Jacob and Esau in regard to their future. By faith, Jacob, when he was dying, blessed each of Joseph's sons and worshipped as he leaned on the top of his staff" (Heb. 11:20–21).

Blessings are significant for couples and families. It is an occasion when a wife and children can receive God's favor through the husband and father's priestly ministry. The Aaronic blessing is central for couple and family blessings. One of God's commands to the priest and the household heads is to pronounce blessings. God wants to bless his people. When the husband or head of household pronounces the Aaronic blessings, God promises to put his name on the recipients and bless them. The husband declares the Word; the Lord imparts the blessings:

"The LORD bless you and keep you; the LORD make his face shine on you and be gracious to you; the LORD turn his face toward you and give you peace…and I will bless them" (Deut. 6:22–27).

Christian husbands and fathers can reclaim this rich heritage in the fabric of Hebraic culture. The Scripture tells us that after returning from ministering before the Ark of the Covenant, "David returned home to bless his family" (1 Chron.16:43). It is God's command and the divine privilege of a husband to bless his wife and family and be abundantly blessed himself. The Lord assures husbands and fathers that "whoever brings blessing will be enriched, and one who waters will himself be watered" by the Lord (Prov. 11:25, ESV).

Leadership at the Family Altar

A family altar is a designated place in the home for regularly scheduled meetings to commune with, honor, and worship the Lord. The altar is the sacred center for spiritual growth and development for the family. The family altar is the nucleus of the family's spiritual life. All aspects of a husband's calling to his wife and family are essential, but marital success is rooted and established in Christ (Col. 2:6–7). Build an altar. Spiritual practices are critical to marriage success. It is needful to reiterate the marriage research findings on the foundations of marital oneness related to spiritual engagement.

In 1997, a Gallup poll commissioned by the National Association of Marriage Enhancement revealed findings that couples who engage in spiritual disciplines significantly increase the prospect of marriage success. The data showed that the divorce rate among couples who pray together was 1 out of 1,152. That is less than 1 percent!

In 2007–2008, the Barna Group conducted studies on divorce rates in America. The research reported that Christians are just as likely to divorce as are non-Christians. The study further confirmed its findings through tracking studies conducted each year.

Other studies have found that divorce rates differ significantly between nominal Christians and those who reported as regularly engaging with their faith. Research from Focus on the Family found that the factor that makes the difference in marriage longevity is religious commitment and practice. Such religious behaviors and attitudes include a combination of regular weekly church attendance, Bible reading, praying privately and together, and commitment to faith. Focus on the Family found that Christian couples who practice such activities show significantly lower divorce rates than mere church members and unbelievers.

Therefore, what conclusion can we draw? The evidence is clear. Marital success is rooted in authentic spiritual engagement with God. Couples who diligently engage in faith practices together, including Bible reading, prayer, reading and listening to material for spiritual growth, and church attendance, significantly increase their prospects for marital success. The Scriptures have also made this truth abundantly clear (Josh. 1:7–8, 2 Pet. 1:3). God commissioned the husband to lead in establishing an altar in their home. Its influence will live on in future generations. Your children, their children, and their children's children will rise up and call you blessed (Prov. 22:6).

Leadership That Cherishes Her

The Lord communicated the ideal marriage with love and respect in a prophetic reference to the relationship with Himself, the Bridegroom, and Israel, his bride:

> And it shall be at that day, says the Lord that thou shall call me Ishi [my husband]; and shall call me no more Baali [master and Lord]. For I will take away the names of Baalim out of her mouth, and they shall no more be remembered by their name. (Hos. 2:16–17, KJV, parentheses added)

Ishi refers to the God of Israel. It translates to "my husband," alluding to a relationship of respect, patience, kindness, gentleness, and affection. Baali was a pagan god signifying a harsh affiliation dominated by a spirit of fear, stern authority, subjection, and lordship. These characteristics are antithetical to love and respect. Jehovah assured His people that his relationship between himself, the Bridegroom, and Israel, His bride was different. Ishi epitomizes respect, warmth, and tender affection. These virtues suggest a protective, caring, and respectful relationship between a husband and wife.

One of my clients, Jessie (not her real name), was so enamored by the understanding of Ishi that she sometimes calls her husband, Ishi. She said that her husband, Carl (not his real name), had grown to live the part over time. Carl's "Ishi" nature had created relationship security in their marriage. Like Sarah, who honored Abraham and called him lord, Jessie felt secure submitting to Carl's leadership.

Abraham had a marriage with Sarah that alluded to an "Ishi"-type relationship of respect, kindness, tenderness, and affection. These virtues produced a healthy environment of marital security, affirmed by the testimony left by Sarah and recorded by the apostle Peter:

> For this is the way the holy women of the past who
> put their hope in God used to adorn themselves.
> They submitted themselves to their own husbands,
> like Sarah, who obeyed Abraham and called him her
> lord. You are her daughters if you do what is right
> and do not give way to fear (1 Pet. 3:5–6).

Loving your wife in an "Ishi" relationship is a sacred privilege given by God. To be devoted to your spouse is a directive from the mouth and heart of God (Eph. 5:25–26). There is no demarcation line between loving God and loving your spouse. Caring for your partner is a manifestation of your love for God (Matt. 22:37–39). When you unconditionally love your mate, you love God (Matt.

25:40). The more you grow in Christ, the greater your capacity to love your wife and please God. God loves through us in caring for our spouse, giving us the desire and the strength to do what pleases Him: "Husbands, love your wives as just Christ loves the Church and gave himself up for her" (Eph. 5:25).

Chapter 14

The Ministry of the Covenant Wife
Gracefully Devoted to God and Family

A Holy Calling

*T*he ministry of the covenant wife is God's plan for the role of a wife in the Christian family. This chapter describes God's model for marriage from the wife's perspective. It outlines the covenant wife's scriptural role and responsibilities in marriage and family ministry. It should be the goal of every wife to bring glory to God in fulfilling the biblical mandate of the covenant wife. This chapter outlines the foundational roles of the covenant wife in executing the functions of her office. Marriage launches a woman into a covenant relationship with her husband and God's calling to marriage ministry. A Christian woman who enters marriage has the sacred duty with her husband to represent the love of Christ and the Church.

Marriage is answering the sacred call from God to embark on ministry with Christ as the supreme head of the union. God did not leave the role of the wife to chance and circumstances. When a person enters employment with an organization, there is a written job description. Likewise, God penned a job description for the vocation of a wife. He also defines the role of mother for the wife who assumes that position. God's divine power has given to spouses all they need through knowledge to find success in marriage and family life (2 Pet. 1:3).

The holy orders for marriage ministry come from God, who officiated the first wedding and wrote the manual for marriage success (Gen. 1:22–24). This manual, the Holy Bible, has structural and interactional features for the harmonious functioning of marriage. The role of the wife is purposed to be a blessing to her husband and bring glory to God.

The Divine Headship of Marriage

Marriage is a sacred institution with the divine headship of Jesus Christ. The Scriptures outline the principles that govern the organizational structure in the Christian family. It is a system created to function "properly and in order" (1 Cor. 14:40, NLT). The marriage leadership design is not of earthy origin. The marital institution has a divine order of governance where Christ is the head of the husband, and the husband is the head of the wife (1 Cor.11:3).

The Scriptures counsel husbands to love their wives as Christ loves the Church and gave Himself for her. Husbands must exercise their leadership role in the spirit of love. Wives must align with the divine order in following their husbands' leadership (Col. 3:18).

The apostle Paul counsels wives "to be submissive to their husbands" so that "they will not bring shame on the Word of God" (Titus 2:5, NLT). A husband's submission to Christ and a wife's collaboration with her husband's leadership are spiritual issues. Couples are ultimately accountable to God for their decisions in marriage. The supreme authority in the marriage institution is Jesus.

Therefore, a wife can only honor and respect her husband when she first submits to Christ in all things. A husband can only lead and love his wife as Christ loves the Church when he willingly surrenders to Christ in all things. Only then can a husband and wife be adequately positioned to pursue married oneness productively.

Role of the Wife: Pathways in Loving Your Husband

Successful marriages are the outcome of spiritual ways and means. God instituted the wife's role as the foundational pathway in loving her husband. The wife's role is the primary way God constituted for her to take care of her husband. Take care of her husband, you ask? This concept came to the forefront of my mind due to an encounter with two clients.

Claudia and Harry (not their real names) came in for their third session. The couple was in their mid-twenties and married for about two years, with one child. As soon as we prayed and Claudia settled down, she said with frustration in her voice: "Dr. Wilson, what my husband needs is a mother to take care of him." Harry remained silent. Harry grew up in a traditional Judeo-Christian home, and an older sister raised Claudia. I probed what exactly Harry wanted that she characterized him as needing a mother. Claudia continued, "Would you believe that I asked Harry to season some fish, and he was clueless?" Taking her inquiry as a rhetorical question, I conveniently took the Fifth and nodded, for I was no more of a chef than Harry.

In conclusion, Harry did need a "mother," and Claudia desperately needed help. Harry wanted Claudia to manage the home, meet their child's needs, and carry out the domestic responsibilities that his mother did. This situation was in light of Claudia being a full-time bank teller, unlike Harry's mother, a full-time homemaker. A new counseling issue emerged. Claudia was overwhelmed and stressed with double duty as a homemaker and bank teller. Harry was not equipped to perform some domestic duties Claudia requested. He also became fully aware that Claudia was holding down two jobs. The problem was now defined. They agreed to discuss the issues and were open to gradual changes in their positions per God's principles as feasible.

Together with the husband, the chief function of the wife is to *shamar* the home, that is, to guard over, preserve, protect, and exercise diligent care. Like the covenant husband, God predetermined the role of the covenant wife. God has prepared the good work of marriage beforehand that spouses may "run with perseverance the race marked out" for them (Eph. 2:10, Heb. 12:1). God structures the Christian marriage to function to produce optimum marital fulfillment.

The covenant wife's primary role is a homemaker. It is an all-encompassing family vocation that affects multiple generations with eternal significance. The Oxford dictionary describes a vocation as "a person's main occupation, especially regarded as particularly worthy and requiring great dedication." The covenant wife manages her household affairs to secure stability, harmony, and prosperity for the family (Titus 2:5, 1 Tim. 5:14, Prov. 31:27). The covenant wife also operates as a family caregiver and nurturer (Prov. 31:10–31), childhood educator (Titus 2:4-5), and various leadership initiatives within and outside the home (Prov. 31:10–31).

The role of the covenant wife is in no way an easy path in today's contemporary society, where the world ridicules her calling to motherhood in the home and exalts promotion and achievement in a competitive marketplace economy. It can be heartrending for some wives and mothers who desire to honor God by adopting His divine plan but face a formidable world system that denigrates godly motherhood.

James and Natasha (not their real names) were in their early thirties. In our conversation, they expressed their frustration about their situation that they both work full time. James was deeply concerned that his income alone was insufficient for the family needs and that it would take three years of part-time evening classes for him to complete his training at a technical institute. It meant that they had to continue keeping the twins at the childcare center. The twins were one-and-a-half years old. Natasha lamented being "desperate to be at home with the boys." We looked at several options. The truth is, there was no simple answer.

The wife's home management role is progressive, always moving toward God's ideal plan for the family (Prov. 4:18). Embracing God's plan for marriage and family gives the work of marriage direction, purpose, and eternal significance (Matt. 6:19–20).

Shaping Civilization

Wives are keepers of the home and family. Keepers of the home are not limited to mean keepers of the house. House is the building; home is a human institution and the cornerstone of society. The word "keep" means "to guard." Wives are the immediate guardians of the home and family. They are co-guardians with their husbands of the values, traditions, precepts, and principles that establish the home and family for their children and the continuity of righteous generations.

The family is the foundational unit of civilization. The priority of the covenant wife is to create a godly home. She establishes a home that nourishes family life and protects it from the ungodly influences of the world. The covenant wife creates a secure, nurturing, and harmonious home environment for her husband, herself, and children. A mother raises her children to be responsible citizens, carrying on a godly heritage to fulfill God's purpose for her family's future generations (Mal.2:15).

Motherhood

One of Satan's prime purposes is to destroy the family and stop God's command to be fruitful and multiply. A mother feeds, protects, and cares for her unborn child until the time of delivery. The devil's first attempt to attack the family is to abort life before full term and birth. The enemy has moved our courts to codify

Satan's plan into law. After delivery, the enemy's second attempt is to influence society to scoff at mothers who adopt the biblical Judeo-Christian culture of motherhood. These mothers seek to take their children to the full term of adulthood through dedicated feeding with God's Word, protecting through intercession, and fulfilling social and emotional needs through maternal love, training, and bonding to godly character formation. The devil's most recent, subtle, and subversive move is to redefine mothers as "birthing people." Motherhood implies a primary vocation as a life process, while birthing people infer motherhood as an event.

Generative Parenting

God desires a husband and wife to raise godly offspring for their joy and the glory of God. Mothers are involved with more of the daily hands-on raising of children. They instruct and model biblical values, precepts, principles, and practices. The Lord requires parents to teach His Word to their children:

> Fix these words of mine in your hearts and minds;
> tie them as symbols on your hands and bind them
> on your foreheads. Teach them to your children,
> talking about them when you sit at home and when
> you walk along the road, when you lie down and
> when you get up (Deut. 11:18–19).

The implications here are strikingly evident. Motherhood, scripturally and ideally, is a full-time career achieved by a dedicated presence for children. The capable wife is always industrious, for her "lamp does not go out at night" (Prov. 31:18). The principle espoused here is that the virtuous and capable wife is diligent in meeting the needs of her husband and family. The Lord charges parents to instill His Word into children in all situations, whether verbal instructions, visual teaching, or modeling behaviors. The Lord intends that a parent's godly lifestyle be generative.

It is evident that some couples cannot immediately achieve God's parenting ideal due to financial constraints. But can couples be primary and supplemental income families and still pursue God's purpose? I counsel my clients to be practical in planning, but I also say, "Be it unto you according to your faith." There are myriads of opportunities in our modern economy and technological society. The "virtuous woman" in Proverbs 31 provided a supplemental income for her family while practicing biblical motherhood. Her business activities were always contributory to her home and family mission. Her priority was continually establishing a productive and harmonious home to nurture and facilitate growth and development. If you would like to enjoy a good read on the life of a homemaker, please see *Stay Home, Stay Happy: 10 Secrets to Loving At-home Motherhood* by best-selling author Rachael Campos-Duffy, listed in the bibliography.

Honoring God: Respecting Your Husband

As we previously discussed, the husband functions as the head of the Christian family. The wife honors the Lord and respects her husband by recognizing his leadership role, "so that the Word of God will not be dishonored" (Titus 2:4–5, emphasis added):

- "But I want you to realize the head of every man is Christ, and the head of the woman is man, and the head of Christ is God" (1 Cor. 11:3).

- "Wives, submit to your husbands, to your own husbands as you do to the Lord. For the husband is the head of the wife as Christ is the head of the Church, his body, of which he is the Savior. Now as the Church submits to Christ, so wives should submit to their husbands in everything. Husbands love your wives, just as Christ loved the Church and gave himself up for her" (Eph. 5:22–25).

- "Wives, submit yourselves to your husbands, as is fitting in the Lord. Husbands, love your wives, and do not be harsh with them" (Col. 3:18–19).

- "This was the kind of beauty seen in the holy women who lived many years ago. They put their hope in God. They also obeyed their husbands. Sarah obeyed her husband, Abraham. She respected him as the head of the house. You are her children if you do what is right and do not have fear" (1 Pet. 3:5–6, NLV).

Mutual Respect

A wife cannot fully love her husband without respecting him, for "love is patient and kind. Love is not jealous or boastful or proud or rude" (1 Cor.13: 4–5, NLT). Respect is subsumed in love. To respect is to love. A covenant husband's need for respect is as critical as his wife's. A husband's need for respect in marriage is more associated with his wife's perspective and responses to his work and leadership in the home (Eph. 5:22–24). A covenant wife's need for respect is more aligned with her perception of her worth concerning her family role and her husband's love and confidence in her (Prov. 31:11, 28).

I have found that most men are usually hurt and angry over overt disrespect or lack of respect from their wives. This response can be from a bruised self-image when a wife does not recognize the principles and precepts that define the biblical role of the husband.

A wife typically responds to disrespect with feelings of hurt and sometimes self-esteem and identity issues. This response is interpreted principally from feeling unloved and devalued when disrespected by her husband. As I previously mentioned, I have had more wives complain of a lack of respect from their husbands than husbands have of their wives. I am also aware that men generally are hesitant to speak in counseling about not being respected by their wives.

When spouses respect each other, they develop confidence in their roles and find security in their relationship. Respect reveals a perception of value in the marital relationship. Mutual and equal respect is a biblical precept at the core of the marriage union (1 Pet. 3:7, Eph. 5:33). The need for respect is at the nucleus of the human heart irrespective of gender.

Loving your husband is a sacred privilege given by God. To be devoted to your husband comes from the heart of God (Eph. 5:33). There is no demarcation line between loving God and loving your husband. Caring for your husband manifests your love for God (Matt. 22:37–39). When you love your spouse, you love God (Matt. 25:40). The more you grow in Christ, the greater your capacity to love your husband and please God, who loves through us, "giving us the desire and the power to do what pleases him" (Phil. 2:13, NLT).

Partnering with Your Husband

The Word of God counsels the Christian wife to be submissive to their husband. The word "submission" is translated from the Greek word *hupotasso*. It was a military term meaning to align with a leader and follow in an orderly manner. When applied to civilian use, it is a voluntary act of cooperation in assuming responsibility. It also means to yield out of respect and or affection. No institution, including marriage, can succeed and, in some cases survive, without an orderly organizational system and leadership.

A wife must first submit in all things to Christ Jesus as head of the marriage union to properly align with her husband's leadership. A wife's submission to her husband's leadership is not coerced. It is *hupotasso*—your voluntary submission to your husband out of respect and affection for him and reverence to Christ. Sarah voluntarily called her husband, Abraham, her lord (leader), because of her respect and affection for him and her reverence for God. She was able to honor him due to her humble disposition before God (1 Pet. 3:6).

The Scriptures beautifully describe the covenant wife as crowning her husband, as she assumes responsibility, cooperates with his leadership, and affirms his position (Prov. 12:4). What if the husband is not a believer? Wives are advised to trust God in living a pure and godly life that their husbands may be won over by their good example (1 Pet. 3:1–3, 5).

The Virtuous and Capable Wife

The wife of Proverbs 31 is God's portrait of a "virtuous and capable wife" (Prov. 31:10, NLT). Other Bible translations describe her as "a truly good wife" (CEV), of "noble character" (CSB), and with a "strong character" (GWT), to name a few.

The capable wife of Proverbs is an ordinary woman with impressive character traits (Prov. 31:10). She is a diligent and morally upright wife (Prov. 31:30). She is engaged in fulfilling her marital and family role in excellence, not necessarily perfection. It is the joy of the virtuous wife to walk in God's will, to do the good work of marriage and family, which God prepared in advance for her (Eph. 2:10).

Let us now explore some of the principles that characterize the capable wife. She is a liberated woman. She carries on entrepreneurial activities from home and the marketplace (Prov. 31:14). She is successful in her trading and investments, even buying real estate property with her earnings (Prov. 31:16–18). Her profits were probably substantial in some seasons. She also engages in designing and making clothing (Prov. 31:24). The capable wife is a successful person, such that she hires housekeepers as she executes her responsibilities (Prov. 31:15). Her husband is pleased with her initiatives and creativity in managing the family institution.

First Priority: God and Family

The priority of the capable wife is family. Her many ventures contribute to her primary mission of looking over her household affairs (Prov. 31:27). Her activities in the home are exemplary. She manages her home and family with great competence that her husband is pleased and has complete confidence in her capabilities (Prov. 31:11). He does not worry. Consequently, her husband's reputation is partly known for his wife's excellent character and work that facilitates his success in his career and community service (Prov. 31:23, 31).

The capable wife has complete freedom of her time. She is not constrained by employment that restricts her availability to her family and community. She trusts in her husband, and her ultimate source is the Lord. She is free to generously give her earnings to the poor in her community outreach (Prov. 31:20).

One of my young clients skillfully weaved her professional education as an accountant into substantial earnings while prioritizing her family. She occasionally hired help for household chores but reserved raising her children at home as a personal responsibility. She remarked that God had blessed her with the gift of being present to impart biblical values into the life of her children.

The virtuous wife raises her children with biblical values and precepts and models the commandments of the Lord (Prov. 31:26). I will not bore you with the volumes of the research that shows the benefits of a child growing up one-on-one with a loving parent in the home. God, of course, always has the perfect plan. We do not need science to support the eternal Word of the omniscient God. I have found that most working wives earnestly desire to replace the daycare in their child's life. I want to note that daycares provide a valuable service to families in our society where the biblical design is not feasible in their season.

Home is Where the Heart Is

The capable wife builds a home that provides a place of comfort, order, and security for her husband and children. Her husband praises her, and her children grow up to bless her (Prov. 31:28). One of my clients gave his wife a beautiful compliment during our discussion on the strength areas of their Prepare Enrich marriage inventory results. The husband described his home as "a solid landing strip I come to at the end of the day, to enjoy pleasant company and a great meal with my family, after flying around at work all day." The wife was a part-time salesperson who prioritized her home and family life.

The priorities of the capable wife are based not only on the temporal but principally on the eternal significance for her family and future generations. It is walking in the good, pleasing, and perfect will of Christ in serving the family that God has entrusted to her. The covenant wife must learn to love her husband and children in the context of her role in the family. It is an art that takes knowledge and practice. The apostle Paul explains that wives need training to love their husbands in the context of their role:

"These older women must train the younger women to love their husbands and their children" (Titus 2:4).

Being the Virtuous and Capable Wife

The covenant wife walks in the Spirit in living biblical values that reflect Christ Jesus. The model of a virtuous and capable wife provides choices for every family's unique circumstances. Wives can have natural gifting and education and training that can be employed creatively for the family's benefit and the glory of God while prioritizing God's ideal. The role of the capable wife can be flexible, predicated upon the stage in the family journey. Couples can modify the family structure and functioning within the biblical principles before they have children, during childhood parenting, and when children reach adulthood. The Bible emphasizes the pre-school and grade school periods as the most crucial stages in God's plan for the role of parents, particularly the nurture and security of the mother's presence in the daily lives of their children:

> Love the LORD your God with all your heart and with all your soul and with all your strength. These commandments that I give you today are to be on your hearts. Impress them on your children. Talk about them when you sit at home and when you walk along the road, when you lie down and when you get up. Tie them as symbols on your hands and bind them on your foreheads. Write them on the doorframes of your houses and on your gates (Deut. 6:5–9),

The capable and virtuous wife "is more precious than rubies; nothing a husband desires can compare with her" (Prov. 3:15). She is "a gentle and quiet spirit, which is of great worth in God's sight" (1 Pet. 3:4). The godly wife is more valuable than rubies and the most precious gift to her husband. Her worth is realized as she seeks to find and walk in God's character and His purpose for the covenant wife.

Marriage and family are always the priority for the virtuous wife. She must please God by submitting her unique family ministry calling to His will. Every wife's situation may be unique. However, the covenant wife always pursues God's purpose for marriage and family. All her entrepreneurial ventures complement her family role, not compete with it. Her lifework is God's approved will, with temporal and eternal significance:

> Therefore, I urge you, brothers and sisters, in view of God's mercy, to offer your bodies as a living sacrifice, holy and pleasing to God—this is your true and proper worship. Do not conform to the pattern of this world, but be transformed by the renewing of your mind. Then you will be able to test and approve what God's will is—his good, pleasing, and perfect will (Rom. 12:1–2).

Chapter 15

Keeping the Joy in Marriage
Repentance, Forgiveness, and Restoration

$\mathcal{W}$e were all spiritually broken and have all fallen short of the glory of God (Rom. 3:23). Thus, there will be offenses in a marriage where the joy and peace of the marital relationship are disturbed. You may pass through troubled waters and walk through the fires of life, but God has promised to lead you as Head of your marriage union (Isa. 43:2).

You may be wounded due to an offense, but remain faithful. The Lord encourages us that the covenant spouse "keeps an oath, even when it hurts, and does not change their mind" about God's work of their marital oneness (Ps. 15:4). The Psalmist says that covenant couples seek to mend the breach and restore the security and harmony in their relationship.

God reconciles marital partners by healing the breach through repentance, forgiveness, and restoration. Facing and resolving relationship challenges is a journey of growth and development where love grows more potent, culminating into ever-increasing oneness (Prov. 4:18). Every decision must be made in light of its eternal significance, that is, in obedience to the Word of God.

The first issue that couples must establish for marital success is agreement on the fundamental biblical principles that govern marriage. The Prophet Amos asks the pivotal question: "Can two people walk together without agreeing on the direction?" (Amos

3:3, NLT). One accord on marital precepts of the Scriptures is the foundation for relationship harmony.

Covenant Spouses Cover Each Other

Probably no other relationship creates more opportunities to forgive than marriage, but covenant spouses give cover to each other:

- "Above all, love each other deeply because love covers over a multitude of sins" (1 Pet. 4:8).

- "A person's wisdom yields patience; it is to one's glory to overlook an offense" (Prov. 19:11).

To cover a multitude of sins is to forgive and keep no record of wrong. In the Old Covenant, God covered transgressions by the sinner's faith in God through the blood of an animal (Heb. 10:4). In the New Covenant, Jesus took away our sins (1 Jn. 3:5). Spouses cover each other's offenses through forgiveness (Prov. 10:12). Jesus blots out the sins and takes them away on repentance. Covenant spouses cover by forgiveness and keep no record of wrong (Matt. 18:15-17).

But who should initiate the reconciliation process? The apostle Paul outlines the principle that applies to reconciling sinners to Christ. This principle extends into working through differences toward marriage reconciliation. God instructed both the offender and offended to initiate reconciliation. God said that it is the responsibility of the husband or wife, regardless of who committed the offense, to begin the restoration process:

- "If another believer sins against you, go privately and point out the offense. If the other person listens and confesses it, you have won that person back" (Matt. 18:15, NLT).

- "All this is from God, who reconciled us to himself through Christ and gave us the ministry of reconciliation; that God was reconciling the world to himself in Christ, not counting people's sins against them. And he has committed to us the message of reconciliation" (2 Cor. 5:18-19).

The first step toward reconciliation is repentance. Biblical repentance in the context of marriage involves the recognition that one has committed an offense against God and one's spouse. This understanding leads to godly sorrow and remorse. This contrition produces confession and a desire to ask for forgiveness (2 Cor.7:10).

Confession acknowledges the transgression against God and one's spouse. At the same time, the husband or wife request God's forgiveness and cleansing (1 Jn 1:9). Biblical repentance involves a change of mind and heart that generates a behavior adjustment in the opposite direction (Acts 3:19).

Repentance Begins with God

True biblical repentance begins with recognizing that the wrongs committed against one's spouse are first sins against God. After committing adultery with Bathsheba, King David confessed that his sin was first against God, declaring, "Against you and you only have I sinned, and done what is evil in your sight" (Ps. 51:4). David was not suggesting that he had not sinned against Bathsheba. David was implying that he had, above all, sinned against God.

Joseph in Egypt responded to temptation from Potiphar's wife by acknowledging that yielding to sin would be principally a transgression against God when responding to his temptress:

"No one is greater in this house than I am. My master has withheld nothing from me except you because you are his wife. How then could I do such a wicked thing and sin against God?" (Gen. 39:9).

Another example is the parable of the prodigal son, who left his home to live a wasteful and immoral life. When he returned to his father, he repented by putting God first in the order of confession, saying, "Father, I have sinned against heaven and against you" (Lk. 15:21).

Brokenness

True repentance must come from a disposition of brokenness before God and one's spouse. God honors the humility of brokenness. Brokenness breeds empathy. Repentance should involve compassion toward one's spouse, even as Jesus feels our pain (Matt. 9:36). The following passages exemplify the spirit of true repentance:

- "My sacrifice, O God, is a broken spirit; a broken and contrite heart you, God, will not despise" (Ps. 51:17).

- "'Even now,' declares the Lord, 'return to me with all your heart, with fasting and weeping and morning. Rend your heart and not your garments. Return to the Lord your God, for he is gracious and compassionate, slow to anger and abounding in love'" (Joel 2:12–13).

Empathy

Entering your spouse's feelings can be a part of the healing process. At times the lack of empathy can delay the process of emotional healing in couples. Two of my clients, a married couple, typify this situation. Jerry and June (not their real names) came in for counseling because of infidelity. Jerry had voluntarily confessed to June about a twelve-year secret affair. During counseling, he expressed his regret, asked for forgiveness, and assured June that he had turned around his life. June forgave him.

However, June and Jerry kept coming back every week, rehashing the story. June was not at peace. June was not experiencing closure even though we went through all the aspects of repentance and forgiveness with prayer.

During one session, Jerry asked to see me alone the following week. We discussed June's pain and her faithfulness to him at that session. For the first time, I saw Jerry become very emotional and brought almost to tears, such that he left before the hour was up.

I saw them a month later. June was happy. She did not relate the full extent of Jerry's emotional response at home but enough to perceive that he was remorseful. Jerry had identified with June and shared in her pain. She felt as one with him. This meeting was their last session.

The Holy Spirit had moved upon Jerry's heart to share June's burden exemplifying the Word to "carry each other's burdens, and in this way, you fulfill the law of Christ" (Gal. 6:2). The law of Christ is the law of love, to love your neighbor as yourself. The Holy Spirit stirred the love of God in Jerry's heart upon experiencing the depth of June's emotional pain. The Holy Spirit breached the emotional gap between Jerry and June. Jerry's submission to God and June released the Spirit's healing and restored the joy to their marital relationship (Eph. 5:21, Jm. 5:16, Ps. 23:3).

Confession

Confession is the first step with your spouse in the reconciliation process. Confession is acknowledging wrongdoing without making excuses and being specific in naming the transgression:

"Therefore, confess your sins to each other and pray for each other so that you may be healed. The prayer of a righteous person is powerful and effective" (Jm. 5:16).

The Lord calls on Christian couples to pray for each other following the act of confession to receive God's healing. Spouses should appeal to Jesus Christ, the divine head of the marital union, to lead the restoration proceedings. Jesus is the "Wonderful Counselor" and "Prince of Peace" (Isa. 9:6), who leads couples on the road to authentic repentance, forgiveness, and restoration (Jn. 16:13).

Seeking Forgiveness

Following confession comes requesting forgiveness. Requesting forgiveness is expressing sorrow for one's transgression and politely asking forgiveness. Your mind and heart must be remorseful. Your mate must know and feel that you are genuinely sorry and share their pain. "I am sorry" is not enough. This version would be better instead, "I am so sorry for the hurt I caused you with my disrespectful words. I commit by God's grace to honor you from this day forward. Would you please forgive me?" This procedure is the basics of seeking forgiveness, which sometimes requires in-depth discussion and professional counseling.

Granting Forgiveness

Granting forgiveness can be a painful and challenging task for some Christians. Unforgiveness bears bitter roots that defile the one who refuses to forgive and those within their sphere of influence, including spouses, children, relatives, and friends (Heb. 12:15). God has entrusted every Christian with the ministry of reconciliation. The Holy Spirit enables the victory of forgiveness and transformation. The Holy Spirit enables Christians to forgive authentically (2 Cor. 5:18). The following Scripture passages contain the fundamental principles that encapsulate the essence of forgiveness. Please read slowly and meditate on each one:

- **"Christians are to forgive one another:** "Be kind and compassionate to one another, forgiving each other, just as in Christ God forgave you" (Eph. 4:32).

- **We are to forgive as Christ forgave us:** "Bear with each other and forgive one another if any of you has a grievance against someone. Forgive as the Lord forgave you" (Col. 3:13).

- **Forgiveness does not keep account of offense:** "Blessed is the one whose sin the Lord will never count against them" (Rom. 4:8).

- **There are no preconditions for forgiveness:** "But God demonstrates his own love for us in this: While we were still sinners, Christ died for us" (Rom. 5:8).

- **Forgiveness is a debt to pay forward:** "And forgive us our debts, as we also have forgiven our debtors" (Matt. 6:12).

- **Forgiveness is a continuing debt:** "Let no debt remain outstanding, except the continuing debt to love one another, for whoever loves others has fulfilled the law" (Rom. 13:8).

- **Forgiveness is a gift:** "For it is by grace you have been saved, through faith—and this is not from yourselves, it is the gift of God—not by works, so that no one can boast" (Eph. 2:8–9).

- **Receiving forgiveness from God is contingent upon granting forgiveness to others:** "For if you forgive other people when they sin against you, your heavenly Father will also forgive you. But if you do not forgive others their sins, your Father will not forgive your sins" (Matt. 6:14–15).

- **Forgiveness restores the joy in relationships:** "Love prospers when a fault is forgiven, but dwelling on it separates close friends" (Prov. 17:9, NLT).

- **Forgiveness restores your ministry to the Lord:** "Therefore, if you are offering your gift at the altar, and there remember that your brother or sister has something against you; leave your gift there in front of the altar. First, go and be reconciled to them; then come and offer your gift" (Matt. 5:23–24).

Forgiveness and Emotions

It is healthy for the person granting forgiveness to express their emotions, acknowledging anger, grief, disappointment, and hurt to their spouse. Verbalizing repressed feelings is therapeutic, bringing catharsis to the person. The Holy Spirit heals the wounded heart through confession (Jm. 5:16).

The offended partner can also facilitate healing to their spouse. When "I forgive you" is verbalized, the offended spouse is in accord with God, unconditionally releasing their partner from the debt of the offense. We must remember that Jesus forgave our even greater debt (Matt. 18:21–35).

Sometimes a husband or wife may also feel that they have not forgiven their spouse even though they have sincerely forgiven them. At times they question some unwanted and lingering emotions regarding their spouse. Do not despair. At times an emotional wound can take a while to heal.

The forgiveness may be real, but the raw emotion of the offense may plague for a while. God requires us to forgive our "brother or sister from the heart" (Matt. 18:35). The biblical meaning of "heart" is "sincerity" in this context and not in our contemporary sense of emotions. It is to forgive sincerely. Proverbs 23:7 speaks of a person who thinks in his heart. Forgiveness is a sincere decision to release a person from the debt of an offense, to give grace instead of seeking justice. You may not feel the intensity of your affection (*raya* love) toward your spouse due to the pain caused by the wrong, but you can continue to love (*ahava* love) them unconditionally (Rom. 5:5). God heals.

Entrusting to God the Pain of Forgiveness

At times you may experience the pain of deep wounds in your desire to forgive. You are releasing your spouse from debt as a gift of grace. This act of release can start a war between the old self and the renewed spirit (Rom. 7:23). You wrestle with yourself.

The answer is to imitate Christ. Spouses are encouraged to cast their burdens on the Lord, for he cares for them and will sustain them in times of trouble (Ps. 55:22). Couples are urged to entrust themselves to God, who judges justly. Jesus embodies this trust in God. When they hurled insults at him, he did not retaliate; he made no threats when he suffered. Instead, "He entrusted himself to him who judges justly" (1 Pet. 2:23).

Entrusting yourself to God for healing can take many fervent prayer encounters, wrestling long hours with God. By seeking God's heart, we experience greater depths of his forgiveness. We overcome by reflecting on the Word. We overcome through faith in Jesus and the testimony of his Word that we are loved (Jn. 3:16). A greater revelation of God's forgiveness informs our belief system and deepens our emotional responses to offenses; to forgive as Christ forgave (Col. 3:13). We are being transformed into His likeness.

Restoration comes when we receive the healing power of the grace of the Lord Jesus Christ, the unconditional love of God, and the comforting fellowship of the Holy Spirit (2 Cor. 13:14). God takes away the pain of the offense so that we can freely relate again. Restoration comes when spouses start acting on the decision to forgive, leading to the Holy Spirit's healing of the soul (Ps.

23:3). Actions communicating forgiveness and restitution between spouses facilitate healing and emotional well-being.

Accepting Forgiveness

Sometimes a spouse may experience difficulty accepting forgiveness for a grievous offense, even after repenting to God and receiving genuine forgiveness from their mate. The most common response from the offending spouse is, "I don't deserve it." I have found it helpful to intervene when a person emotionally struggles to receive forgiveness. We usually would discuss Philippians 4:6–7, emphasizing God's peace. I would then verbalize the forgiveness and freedom God has already graciously extended to them (1 Jn. 1:9). I have seen the relief on my clients' faces when I agree with God and their spouse that they are forgiven. I would typically declare:

"John, you are forgiven. Shirley has forgiven you. God has forgiven you and taken away your guilt. Yes, we do not deserve forgiveness. It is Shirley's gift to you. God pardoned you on behalf of His Son Jesus. Receive God's grace."

I do this as needed now during counseling. Humorously, but with gratitude, I sometimes feel like a Catholic priest administering the sacrament of confession.

Restoration

Restoration is the final stage in repairing the breach in marital relationships and returning domestic tranquility to the marriage. Covenant spouses seek to restore each other as Christ has set us an example (Jm. 5:19–20). I would like to pause here to say that forgiveness does not always lead to reconciliation. There are situations where abuse can be too harmful to a spouse to reconcile safely without pastoral guidance or professional Christian counseling.

Encourage Yourself in the Lord

An important rule in marriage is to keep no record of wrong (1 Cor. 13:5). This action involves putting the past behind, for "whoever would foster love covers over an offense" (Prov. 17:9). Paul also admonishes us to forget the past failures, live in the present, and reach for the future in Christ (Phil. 3:13–14).

The model principles for restoration are in the parable of the prodigal son and the father who restored him. In the parable of Luke 15, the son left his father's household, lived a sinful life, and wasted his inheritance. He finally returned home expressing unworthiness. But the father welcomed him with open arms; put a coat upon him, a ring on his finger, and shoes on his feet, symbolizing restoration. These acts of grace restored fellowship and affirmed the son's relationship and position. God the Father does the same for His children when we return to Him. He put a coat upon us, a ring on our finger, and shoes on our feet: forgiving our transgressions, affirming our righteousness standing with Him through His Son Jesus, and restoring fellowship with us. Jesus admonishes us to do likewise (Luke 10:37).

Sometimes couples focus on the shortcomings in their relationship rather than their blessings. This perspective results in a feeling of discontent and discouragement. The apostle Paul advises us "to be content whatever the circumstances" (Phil. 4:11). He also instructs us in the way to find the peace of soul. Paul exhorts us to encourage "one another with psalms, hymns, and songs from the Spirit" and to "always giving thanks to God the Father for everything, in the name of the Lord Jesus" (Eph. 5:19–20). King David knew the secret of contentment when he encouraged himself in the Lord:

"And David was greatly distressed; for the people spake of stoning him, because the soul of all the people was grieved, every man for his sons and for his daughters: but David encouraged himself in the LORD his God" (1 Sam. 30:6, KJV).

At times the spirit of discontent may creep into your marriage. At such times Sherron and I have dedicated an entire devotional time to encourage ourselves in the Lord. We thank God for His blessings on our marriage, family, and Church. Our praise and worship focus on God's goodness. Our prayer session would be exclusively thanksgiving to God for salvation, the Lord's faithfulness, our marriage and family blessings, and many other benefits. The Spirit of gratitude overwhelms us, and God's peace and contentment would cover us (Phil. 4:7).

Loving by Faith and Not by Sight

Your faith in your marriage oneness is faith in God. Choose to believe God's declaration of your oneness over your natural circumstances. There are periods in marriage when we must embrace our oneness tenaciously to ride out the storm. These are the challenging seasons when we cannot perceive oneness in the natural but must trust in Him, who can guard the marital covenant entrusted in Him. During the storm, we love by faith and not by sight (2 Cor. 5:7). Have faith in your union when there seems to be nothing tangible to confirm your oneness. It is recorded in Heaven. The God who cares can keep what you have committed to Him at the marital altar (1 Pet. 5:7).

Remember, our faith is in Him who "makes the clouds his chariots and rides on the wings of the wind" (Ps. 104:3). Be still, "and the Father who knows all hearts" will listen with empathy and strengthen your faith and love in your marital oneness (Rom. 8:27, NLT).

Emotional Wholeness

God is the one who ultimately heals and restores the wounded soul and then leads us in the new path of righteousness (Ps. 23:3).

God cleanses us from our transgression. God promises that if we confess to him, he will forgive our offenses against him and our spouse and cleanse us from the stain of our sin (1 Jn. 1:9). The apostle James also reminds us that when we confess to each other and pray for each other, God will heal the wounded soul of both spouses (Jm. 5:16). On repentance, God revives the joy in our soul and restores our emotional wholeness (Ps. 51:12). There is a balm in Gilead. God heals.

Be Content in Waiting upon the Lord

Your spouse's transformation is a process. Wait on the Lord for your spouse's growth and development. Your spouse may be doing the same for you. God is doing the same for you. Our Lord counsels us to be patient in bearing with one another in love (Eph. 4:20). Be content with your partner's present spiritual and emotional stage as you wait on the Lord. Rest in prayer and thanksgiving, and the Lord will grant you his peace and well-being (Eph. 4:6–7).

Be patient and at peace about the things that only God can change. My father always said that time heals all things. My mother's saying was, "Leave it up to God." Together they were right. If your spouse struggles to change, it may be some emotional or spiritual issue. Give them grace and time. God has given you an abundance of both, more than enough to pay forward:

"His divine power has given us everything we need for a godly life through our knowledge of him, who called us by his own glory and goodness" (2 Pet. 1:3).

So "Wait on the Lord; be of good courage, and he shall strengthen your heart; wait I say, wait on the Lord"! (Ps. 27:14, KJV).

God defines us by his imputed righteousness through Jesus Christ. He characterizes us by our restored present, not by the transgressions he cleansed us from the past. He will portray us by what He has removed in us, not by the breaches along the way. Abraham made some serious breaches in his marital relationship with Sarah, allowing her to be taken twice into the harem of pagan kings to save his life. God was faithful to keep his covenant with him.

Abraham grew in faith and is known as the father of the faithful. His mention in Hebrews 11 never says anything about his failure but highlights his faith. By God's grace, Abraham was a covenant keeper. By God's grace, you can also turn your woundedness into wholeness in Christ. You also can live to enter the Hall of Faith as a covenant keeper with God and your spouse. Love by faith. Let your faith in your Oneness express itself through love as you wait on the Lord (Gal.5:6).

Chapter 16

Covenant Keepers
Faithful and True

his chapter discusses fidelity in marriage, focusing on sexual integrity. Unfortunately, sexual unfaithfulness among Christian couples may be increasing, reflected in my annual cases for the past fifteen years. For most clients, the sexual sin was not solely lust but also Satan's clever schemes of outwitting the spouse involved. Our discussion centers on avoiding moral failures so that husbands and wives can be faithful and true to each other by walking in covenant-keeping sexual integrity. Our victory comes from walking by faith in Him, who is our strength:

"We now have this light shining in our hearts, but we ourselves are like fragile clay jars containing this great treasure. This makes it clear that our great power is from God, not from ourselves" (2 Cor. 4:7, NLT).

We are not alone in this journey. When we turn to God, we find his eyes are on us and ready to show himself strong on our behalf (2 Chron. 16:9). Walking out covenant marriage and living our Christian life is, in essence, the same. There is no differentiation. We are in covenant with our spouse. But we are also in covenant with God through our salvation and wedding vows. If we break covenant with our spouse, we break covenant with God. We cannot maintain the purity of sexual integrity in spirit, soul, and body apart from God:

"May God himself, the God of peace, sanctify you through and through. May your whole spirit, soul, and body be kept blameless at the coming of our Lord Jesus Christ" (1 Thess. 5:3).

Sexual Integrity

Adultery and fornication are sexual pleasures outside of marriage. All sin begins in the heart. Jesus said that "anyone who looks at a woman lustfully has already committed adultery with her in his heart" (Matt. 5:28). Jesus alerts us to watch and pray that we do not fall into temptation, for "the spirit is willing, but the flesh is weak" (Matt. 26:41). Being vigilant is crucial (Eph. 6:10–18). However, the most effective weapon is staying pure by "obeying the truth" of God's Word (Matt. 26:41). Marriage is a blessing from God that requires those given this trust to remain faithful (1 Cor. 4:2).

Christ, Our First Love

The first consideration in walking in the path of moral purity is our relationship with God, for "his divine power has given us everything we need for a godly life" (2 Pet. 1:3). God "has given us the victory through our Lord Jesus Christ" (1 Cor. 15:57). Our fidelity begins with our faithfulness to God. He is our first love. Loving God is the first line of defense in remaining faithful to our spouse. Jesus confirmed this truth when the Pharisees inquired which is the greatest commandment. Jesus replied:

"'Love the Lord your God with all your heart and with all your soul and with all your mind.' This is the first and greatest commandment. And the second is like it: 'Love your neighbor as yourself'" (Matt. 22:37–39).

We are strong when we are first submitted to God. I have counseled couples who referenced their spouse as the reason that they yielded to temptation in an attempt to minimize the gravity of their actions. This explanation is Satan's clever scheme to "outwit us" (2 Cor. 2:11). There is no excuse for sin, for we are drawn away and enticed by our own desires (Jm. 1:14). God strengthens us when we turn to Him first in the face of temptation (2 Chron. 16:9). Our heart also moves to guard our relationship with the lover of our soul. Our relationship with God is our strength, for our intimacy with Jesus constrains us from sin (2 Cor. 5:14).

Crucified with Christ

The marriage covenant is the spiritual bedrock of fidelity. The Christian marriage covenant includes Christ, the husband, and the wife. Couples can informally and periodically reaffirm their covenant with God and with each other to deepen their dependence on God and strengthen their resolve to be faithful and true to each other.

The first step in living the life of an overcomer is to crucify the flesh. To crucify the flesh is to deny the self of its inordinate desires and lust. The Word of God declares that Christians "have crucified the flesh with its passions and desires" (Gal. 5:24). The apostle Paul reiterated that to the Romans when he stated that our old self was crucified with Christ Jesus so that we would no longer be enslaved to sin (Rom. 6:6). Please note the past tense in this verse. Spiritually, we were crucified and buried with Jesus. That is the finished work of the Spirit.

But there is also the crucifixion of the flesh in the present continuous tense. We take up our cross daily:

> If you are living according to the impulses of the flesh, you are going to die. But if you are living by the power of the Holy Spirit, you are habitually putting to death the sinful deeds of the body; you will live forever (Rom. 8:13, Amp).

Walking in the Spirit

The crucifixion of the flesh and walking in the Spirit are two sides of the same coin. We crucify the flesh when we walk in the Spirit. Walking in the spirit is being obedient to God by choice through the empowerment of the Holy Spirit:

- "So I say, walk by the Spirit, and you will not gratify the desires of the flesh. For the flesh desires what is contrary to the Spirit, and the Spirit what is contrary to the flesh. They are in conflict with each other so that you are not to do whatever you want. But if you are led by the Spirit, you are not under the law" (Gal. 5:16–18).

- "We know that our old sinful selves were crucified with Christ so that sin might lose its power in our lives. We are no longer slaves to sin. For when we died with Christ, we were set free from the power of sin" (Rom. 6:6–7, NLT).

To walk in the Spirit is to embrace the truth of our dominion over sin. We live in obedience to God by faith, "who gives us the desire and power to do what pleases him" (Phil. 2:13, NLT). We are no longer slaves to our fleshly desires. The Spirit empowers us to choose righteousness over moral compromise.

God's Spirit is the central command center in the born-again Christian that submits to the will of God. When the believer surrenders to God, the Holy Spirit operates and controls the believer's spirit. The believer's spirit leads the soul, and the body responds to the soul. The Christian submitted to Christ has the power to choose utmost propriety (Rom. 6:20–22).

Be Filled with the Spirit

How are we enabled to walk in the Spirit? We are empowered in our relationship with Jesus Christ through His Spirit (Jon 15:5). Saint Paul informs us of the means: to be filled with the Spirit. He counsels us not to be filled with wine but to "keep on being filled with the Spirit" (Eph. 5:18, ISV). Filled with wine implies that much alcohol affects our actions. Filled with the Spirit signifies that the Holy Spirit influences our behavior. In the context of Ephesians 5, we are commanded to be filled with the Spirit continually. We achieve this through our daily fellowship with God in worship with thanksgiving, meditating on the Word, and communion in prayer (Eph. 4:12, 5:18-20, & James 5:16).

The outcome is a surrendered life nurtured and governed by the Holy Spirit into ever-increasing intimacy with God. We have victory over sin as we are being "completely filled with the very nature of God" (Eph.3:19, GNT). Evangelist D L Moody was once asked why he encouraged Christians to be filled constantly with the Holy Spirit. "Well," he said, "I need a continual infilling because I leak!" Pointing to a water tank that leaked, he continued, "I'm like that!" he said. You got the point. Keep on being filled with the Holy Spirit daily.

Overcoming Temptation

This section will examine some principles and strategies in overcoming sexual temptation. The most debilitating position in the battle over moral issues is to put our confidence in ourselves. The Word of God admonishes us:

- "Watch and pray so that you will not fall into temptation. The spirit is willing, but the flesh is weak" (Matt. 26:41).

- "For it is we who are the circumcision, we who serve God by his Spirit, who boasts in Christ Jesus, and who put no confidence in the flesh" (Phil. 3:3).

- "We are human, but we don't wage war as humans do. We use God's mighty weapons, not worldly weapons, to knock down the strongholds of human reasoning and to destroy false arguments. We destroy every proud obstacle that keeps people from knowing God. We capture their rebellious thoughts and teach them to obey Christ" (2 Cor.10:3–5, NLT).

Draw Near to God

The apostle James instructs us on how to be victorious over Satan, the world, and the sinful desires of the flesh:

- "Submit yourselves, then, to God. Resist the devil, and he will flee from you. Come near to God, and he will come near to you" (Rom. 4:7–8).

- "Draw near to God, and He will come near to you" (Jm. 4:8).

The first act in resisting sexual temptation from the flesh, the world, and the devil is to submit to God. We resist temptation when the Holy Spirit leads in humble surrender to God. We are submitted to God when He is Lord of our lives. We reflect a humble disposition in obedience when Jesus is Lord of our lives, in obedience to His Word.

When we walk daily in obedience to Christ, we draw near to God, and He draws near to us. We are consequently enabled and empowered to declare our convictions and stand our ground to resist the devil, the world, and the evil inclinations of the flesh. When we employ spiritual weapons, the devil will flee for a season just as he did with Jesus until another opportune time (Lk. 4:16).

We must walk in a lifestyle characterized by obedience and vigilance to live a victorious Christian life.

Drawing near God also implies not having a close relationship with those who may influence you to sin. The Church of God has many saints of high moral integrity with which you can find appropriate fellowship. Do not be misled by the enemy to think that close friendship with those of an immoral lifestyle would not affect you. The Lord cautions us to be careful, for "bad company corrupts good character" (1 Cor. 15:33).

Victory by Faith

The key to victory over infidelity is our faith, "for every child of God defeats this evil world, and we achieve this victory through our faith" (1 Jn. 5:4). It is not how much we strive. It is "fixing our eyes on Jesus the pioneer and perfector of our faith" (Heb. 12:2). This faith is the trust in our Lord Jesus, who can keep us from falling into temptation (Jude 1:24).

Faith develops by hearing the Word of God (Rom. 10:17). "Hearing" in the Hebrew culture is not just perceiving by the natural ear. Hearing is to ponder God's Word and act in obedience to it. Our faith in and love for God corresponds to our obedience to Him and our dependence on Him. When we acknowledge our need, displaying our weakness, the power of Christ works through us, giving us victory over temptation and the devil (2 Cor. 12:9).

How the Lord Jesus Overcame Temptation

Jesus overcame temptation through spiritual warfare utilizing the Word in the Old Covenant. Satan's first temptation to Jesus in the wilderness was to turn stone into bread. Satan tempted him at the point of his need. Jesus had fasted 40 days and 40 nights and was hungry (Matt. 4:1–4). He responded to Satan with the sword of the Spirit, the Word of God, stating that man shall not live by bread alone but on every word that comes from the mouth of God (Matt. 4:4). This passage was a direct quotation of Deuteronomy 8:3.

Satan then asked Jesus to throw himself down from the pinnacle of the temple so that angels would save him. Jesus replied that no one should put the Lord to the test (Matt. 4:7), a quote taken from Deuteronomy 6:16.

Finally, the devil offered Jesus the kingdoms of the world if he would bow down and worship him. Jesus responded that one should worship the Lord God and serve Him only (Matt. 6:10). He again cited the Old Covenant, referring to Deuteronomy 6:13. Jesus understood that "no word of God shall be void of power" (Lk. 1:37, ASV). He weaponized the Word of God.

By using the principles modeled by Jesus, you can defeat temptation. With a life of obedient submission to the Holy Spirit, confess the Word of God about your marriage: that you are no longer two but one (Matt.9:6). By this Christlike act, you can war successfully for your covenant marriage.

Imitate Christ Jesus

The apostle Paul encourages us to imitate Jesus in our Christian walk. Jesus was proactive regarding temptation. He was equipped to overcome the flesh, the world, and the devil. Jesus was obedient to His Fathe, and he studied and memorized the Scriptures. He answered every temptation from Satan by confessing the Word from the Old Testament. Thus, Jesus crucified the flesh, overcame the world, and defeated the devil.

The battle for the soul should not start during the temptation. It begins with a lifestyle of obedience to the Word, preparation, and vigilance. The Word of God was in the heart and on the lips of Jesus. All life experiences begin in the heart, for a person's behavior emanates from his thoughts (Prov.23:7). There are many principles to equip the believer. The following passages are a few examples:

- **Put on God's armor:** "For this reason, take up the whole armor of God so that you may be able to take a stand whenever evil comes. And when you have done everything you could, you will be able to stand firm" (Eph. 6:13–17).

- **Be ready with the Word:** "Pay attention and turn your ear to the sayings of the wise; apply your heart to what I teach, for it is pleasing when you keep them in your heart and have all of them ready on your lips so that your trust may be in the Lord" (Prov. 22:17–19).

- **Vigilance in Prayer:** "Very early in the morning, while it was still dark, Jesus got up, left the house, and went off to a solitary place, where he prayed" (Mk. 1:35).

Jesus diligently prayed, studied, and meditated on the Word. In the Spirit of humble submission, He memorized and applied the the words of the Psalmist, "I have hidden your word in my heart that I would not sin against you" (Psalm 119:11). When temptation came, he wielded the sword of the Spirit, the Word of God, unto victory. Jesus assures us that the Holy Spirit would remind us of the precepts we have learned when temptations come (Jn. 14:26).

Our preparation against temptation also means that we are in fellowship with God. We are developing a relationship of trust and friendship with God. We usually call on those we know and trust when we need help. God responds to relationships as the Psalmist recorded:

> "Because he loves me," says the LORD, "I will rescue
> him; I will protect him, for he acknowledges my
> name. He will call on me, and I will answer him; I

will be with him in trouble, I will deliver him and honor him." (Ps. 91:14–15)

Praying without Ceasing

The Word of God alerts us to pray continuously:

- "Rejoice always, pray without ceasing, in everything give thanks; for this is the will of God in Christ Jesus for you" (1 Thess. 5:16–18, NKJV).

- "And take the helmet of salvation, and the sword of the Spirit, which is the word of God; praying always with all prayer and supplication in the Spirit, being watchful to this end with all perseverance and supplication for all the saints" (Eph. 6:17–18, NKJV).

- "Be anxious for nothing, but in everything by prayer and supplication, with thanksgiving, let your requests be made known to God" (Phil. 4:6, NKJV).

- "Continue earnestly in prayer, being vigilant in it with thanksgiving" (Col. 4:2, NKJV).

Prayer is a powerful and effective tool in our arsenal of spiritual weapons. The Word informs us that "the prayer of a righteous person is powerful and effective" (Jm. 5:16). The Lord urges us to pray continually and pray about everything. The meaning communicated in these verses above is to always be in an attitude of prayer. An attitude of prayer implies a disposition of humble dependence on God, even as a child (Matt. 18:3). A humble attitude of submission to Christ tells of an intimate relationship with God.

Many years ago, my four-year-old son lost his toy car. I could not locate it. He later came to me in tears and said, "Dad, I lost my car. I asked God to tell me where it is. Dad, God knows where it is, but he is not telling me!" Part of his frustration was that God was not telling him. He was troubled about the car but also about his relationship with God. Unfortunately, I don't remember how I handled it, but he never found the car. God has since used Dr. James Dobson's books to wise me up with better responses in parenting.

What is the moral of this story? My son was at a stage of total dependence on me as his earthly father and God his heavenly Father. The minute a problem arose, he looked for help, even for small things. We as Christians should be in complete reliance on our heavenly Father, even as a child. Young children turn to their parents for help when encountering any challenge.

Whenever a temptation arises, Christians should turn to Christ immediately. Prayer redirects our mind away from the problem to faith in the One who has the solution. That means always being in a state of worship. A state of worship is a disposition of submission. That is a "bowed down" mindset unto the Lord. Trust God. It is very difficult to fall into temptation when you are in a state of "praying without ceasing"! You can take this to the bank. Jesus affirmed this truth when he said, "Watch and pray so that you will not fall into temptation" (Matt. 26:41). God has promised:

"Call on me in the day of trouble; I will deliver you, and you will honor me" (Ps. 50:15).

Flee Sexual Immorality

The apostle Matthew metaphorically emphasizes how one should resist sexual temptation. God requires uncompromising and harsh actions against the flesh to maintain moral rectitude:

> You have heard that it was said you shall not commit adultery. But I tell you that anyone who looks at a woman lustfully has already committed adultery with her in her heart. If your right eye causes

you to stumble, gouge it out and throw it away. It
is better for you to lose one part of your body than
for your whole body to be thrown into hell. And if
your right hand causes you to stumble, cut it off and
throw it away. It is better for you to lose one part of
your body than for your whole body to go into hell.
(Matt. 5:27–30).

God's Word is clear that Christians should deal harshly with
sexual temptations. The apostle Paul admonishes us to flee sexual
immorality. God's instructions are not to delay and test your human
strength (Jer. 17:5,7). The apostle Paul counsels us to "keep on run-
ning from sexual immorality" (1 Cor. 6:18, ISV). This verse is in
the present continuous tense, requiring a mental disposition of vigilance and dependence on God. Glorify God: run undignified from
sexual temptation as Joseph did from Potiphar's wife.

The pride of the soul comes before the fall of the flesh. God commands us to flee from sexual sin. This stand denies "the devil an
opportunity to work" in our lives (Eph. 4:27). Victory means living
within principles and boundaries that keep us out of the range of
moral compromise. These standards make no provision for the flesh
(Rom. 13:14).

Marital Boundaries

Joseph, son of the patriarch Jacob, was tested severely in Egypt
under his master, Potiphar. Potiphar's wife tried to seduce Joseph
into sexual sin. When she grabbed his coat to force him into the
act, Joseph ran and left his coat behind, refusing to sin against God
(Gen. 39:6–13). He stood his ground by leaving the scene. Joseph
had set moral boundaries following scriptural guidelines.

One of my clients was in a situation that did not turn out well
because of the lack of established principles and boundaries in his

marriage relationship. He came into counseling with his wife for a moral failure. I believe he was genuinely sorry. His story began when he and two co-workers planned to meet at an apartment to work on a project. The apartment belonged to the team's female member, who my client knew in college and dated briefly.

On the way to the 7:00 p.m. appointment, the other male team member called and said that he could not make it but that the rest of the team should proceed without him. My client was hesitant at first but proceeded on the premise that there was no way anything could happen between him and the young lady. He went to the apartment, and it happened. There was remorse immediately following the sexual act. He was distressed when he entered my office.

Ken and Earlese (not their real names) were engaged. They were both in their mid-twenties and came in for premarital counseling. Earlese was completing her last year in a culinary arts program. In the first session, Earlese wept profusely, and Ken was visibly disturbed. They revealed that they engaged in premarital sex and felt guilt and remorse even after repentance. They had established biblical principles for their relationship that were falling apart. They had not, however, discussed or set any relationship boundaries.

Earlese lived with her parents, and Ken lived in his apartment. The only situation where they privately met was at Ken's place. They decided and committed to having all their dating and social events away from Ken's home and privately engaged daily in fervent prayer. By the fifth session, the situation resolved to a happy ending because they committed to pleasing God. Their joy was restored, and they shortened their engagement period from one year to five months. It was refreshing to see that these two young people's desire to please God overshadowed their emotional and physical passion for each other.

In the not-too-distant past, premarital couples had chaperones. The chaperones served as "walls" to maintain sexual purity. You may not wish to return to that time in history. But you should build your own "walls." Establish boundaries that please God and bless your relationship now and pass on generational blessings.

Personal Boundaries in Leadership

One area that has come to be of great concern to the Church is the moral failure of some pastors and ministry leaders. Every pastor or ministry leader I counseled for moral failure has been in an affair with a congregation member where the leader ministered. The ministers, all men, claimed that their affair was not intentional but was a progression in unwise familiarity with someone that led to the impropriety.

One of the wiles of Satan is to ensnare Christians by pursuing actions because the motive is honorable. This situation is the "right motive, wrong action" trap. Pastor Josh (not his real name) thought that he might help one of his female congregants by giving her a ride to physical therapy once a week. The church member had been in an accident, was temporarily on crutches, and could not drive. Pastor Josh would assist her up to her apartment on dropping her off. This gesture sounds charitable and innocent. Within two months, they had a consensual sexual relationship.

An area that some pastors probably never think of is the issue of personal space and touch. Women react differently in these situations. All women were not created equal in their perception and reaction about personal space and physical contact with the opposite sex.

One of my clients shared that she no longer goes up for prayer at the altar. Her pastor, she said, was too close during ministry. Both of his hands embraced her in a face-to-face light hug during prayer. She related that she cringed with discomfort. Another young lady mentioned that her pastor would put his hand around her lower waist when he prayed for her. It was very uncomfortable for her, but she found it difficult to voice her concern to him. Both of these ladies said that from their experience, their pastors were kind and caring men of outstanding character. Their standing in the community confirms that.

One way to guard against pastoral moral failure is to establish boundaries between the pastor or ministry leader and those they work with or serve. There were no proactive safeguards to avoid moral failures in the ministry organizational structure of the leaders I counseled. The ministers had no established personal boundaries, and the church boards had no guidelines in place for them. These pastors were not following the biblical principles and precepts that safeguard moral integrity. All the ministers were aware of the biblical instructions to avoid moral failure. However, they may not have meditated on them or discussed them with their wives to own those principles as a lifestyle. One way that supports moral integrity is the adoption of the Graham-Pence Principle.

The Graham-Pence Principle

The Graham-Pence Principle seeks to essentially avoid any situation that may lead to moral compromise for oneself or others in our sphere of influence. The Word of God instructs us to "abstain from all appearances of evil" (1 Thess. 5:22, KJV). The appearance of evil can lead to sin. When Christians avoid the appearance of evil, they also set an example for less mature Christians. It avoids any form of impropriety and suspicion. Be vigilant. Satan is subtle in presenting temptation. He begins with a seemingly benign thought, word, or action. The change may be so small that you may hardly notice. Satan is a master at gradualism! He changed Eve's thinking by essentially adding one word to God's instruction. Instead of, "You shall surely die," he said, "You shall not surely die."

The Rev. Billy Graham, during his ministry, pledged not to eat, travel, or meet with a woman other than his wife, Ruth, unless other people were present. It is public knowledge that the late Dr. Billy Graham lived a virtuous life.

In 2017 Vice President Pence made headlines with a media report. In 2002 Vice President Pence asserted that he never eats alone with a woman. He also revealed that he would not attend events having alcohol without his wife, Karen, by his side. It is also reported that Vice president Pence did not have female aides with him whenever he worked late at the White House.

It is refreshing to know that even in Hollywood entertainment, some of God's servants stand tall in upholding standards of moral integrity with boldness, bringing glory to the name of the Lord. Kirk Cameron, for example, has established scriptural boundaries in his acting career that exemplify his zeal for God and his passion and honor for his wife, Chelsea. Kirk does not engage in intimate kissing with co-stars as part of any script. This act of affection he has reserved only for Chelsea.

Reverend Graham, former Vice President Pence, and actor Kirk Cameron have all lived by scriptural principles for moral integrity. They all established safe and respectable boundaries to honor God and their wife of covenant. Couples must periodically discuss, agree, and set practical relationship boundaries based on the immutable Word of God to guard and preserve the sanctity of their sacred union.

Guard Your Heart

The apostle Paul, in a letter to the Corinthians, wrote:

> Now I will answer the questions that you asked in your letter. You asked, "Is it best for people not to marry?" Well, having your own husband or wife should keep you from doing something immoral… To the unmarried and the widows, I say that it is

good for them to remain single, as I am. ...But if they do not have self-control, let them marry, for it is better to marry than to burn with passion (1 Cor. 7:1–2, 7–8 ESV)

As discussed earlier, spouses' first act in maintaining moral rectitude is to build a spiritual fortress. This defense uses spiritual weapons effectively while living according to biblical principles and precepts on marriage. There are also practical and helpful reinforcement strategies to facilitate walking in moral uprightness. The apostle Paul's response to the Corinthian Church quoted above implied that having sexual fulfillment in marriage could be a helpful safeguard against sexual temptation.

A spouse is more likely to be distracted with sexual temptation, whether through the soul or body when extended periods of sexual unfulfilled desires exist in marriage. It is the reason that the Word counsels married couples to meet each other's sexual needs so that Satan will not tempt them because of their lack of self-control (1 Cor. 7:5). Satan attacked Jesus at the point of His need. He asked Him to turn stone into bread after Jesus had fasted 40 days and was hungry. He will also tempt you at the point of your need. Satan is a roaring lion seeking to destroy your marriage (1 Pet. 5:8).

Men especially should guard their eyes because of their propensity to visual stimulation, leading to spiritual adultery. The eyes are generally the window of the soul to sexual lust. The patriarch Job made a covenant with his eyes not to look lustfully at a woman (Job.31:1). Husbands are less likely to have a moral failure when experiencing sexual fulfillment, as expounded in Chapter 10. However, every husband is solely responsible to God and his wife for his moral purity regardless of need and the prevailing circumstances in the marital relationship.

God gives special significance to the heart for its role in maintaining moral integrity in marriage. The book of Proverbs alerts us to "guard your heart above all else, for it determines the course of your life" (Prov. 4:23, NLT).

Women are more likely to be drawn into sexual temptation through their emotions. All of the wives of the couples I counseled fell into sexual sin through an affair that began by sharing personal issues with a compassionate male associate. The infidelity cases started at work or in social environments with social and emotional contact opportunities. Constant engagements with a male associate led to an eroding of boundaries and increased emotional connection. The pattern was verbal sharing at the personal level.

Sharing intimate contents of the heart led first to an emotional attachment and then to emotional infidelity. The heart is the first to fall. It is a slippery slope. Wives are less likely to have a moral failure when they experience sexual wholeness, as expounded in Chapter 9. However, every wife is solely responsible to God and her husband for her moral purity regardless of need or the prevailing circumstances in the marital relationship. Guard your heart. Trust in Him who is able to keep you:

> To him who is able to keep you from stumbling and to present you before his glorious presence without fault and with great joy—to the only God our Savior be glory, majesty, power, and authority, through Jesus Christ our Lord, before all ages, now and forevermore! Amen. (Jude 24–25).

Faithful and True

How can a person live a virtuous life? Two passages in the book of Psalm and Proverbs explains with succinct clarity:

- "How can a young person stay on the path of purity? By living according to your word… I have hidden your word in my heart that I might not sin against you... I meditate on your precepts and consider your ways. I delight in your decrees; I will not neglect your word" (Ps. 119:9–16).

- "Let love and faithfulness never leave you; bind them around your neck, write them on the tablet of your heart. Then you will win favor and a good name in the sight of God and man" (Prov. 3:3–4).

Covenant keepers are faithful and true to God and their spouses. Covenant keepers are covenant lovers who pursue marital oneness by following Jesus, the lover of our soul. The path of marriage oneness is through "the great and awesome God, who keeps his covenant of love with those who love him and keep his commandments" (Neh. 1:5):

For this reason, I kneel before the Father, from whom every family in heaven and on earth derives its name. I pray that out of his glorious riches, he may strengthen you with power through his Spirit in your inner being so that Christ may dwell in your hearts through faith. And I pray that you, being rooted and established in love, may have power, together with all the Lord's holy people, to grasp how wide and long and high and deep the love of Christ, and to know this love that surpasses knowledge—that you may be filled to the measure of all the fullness of God (Eph. 3:14–19).

Chapter 17

The Call for Marriage Reformation
Rebuilding the Ancient Foundations

The Call to Counterculture

Our Father in Heaven calls Christian couples who are exhausted from the burdens of married life to return to Him and His ways and find rest. The Lord is calling all Christian couples to have an abundant marriage experience. The call is to cancel the world culture on marriage, dispelling the darkness with the Light of His Word (Jn. 8:12).

In one of his posts, Dutch Sheets, an internationally known teacher, revealed an insightful interpretation in Matthew 28. He explained that Jesus commissioned the Church to disciple the nations. But instead, he said, the world system has discipled and transformed all aspects of society for the last 30 years. Christ commissioned Christians to "make disciples of all nations" (Matt. 28:19), not the nation make disciples of Christians!

We are the salt of the earth, kingdom influencers of society's institutions, with marriage and family being preeminent (Matt. 5:13). The enemy crept onto marriage so slowly that Christians have hardly noticed the gradual change from the Judeo-Christian precepts to the pattern of the world. The nations have discipled our generation with an infusion of its tenets, principles, and lifestyle. It is God's heart for his bride to displace the world customs within the Church with the culture of the kingdom of God, engendering a heritage of generational blessings:

> Don't copy the behavior and customs of this world, but let God transform you into a new person by changing the way you think. Then you will learn to know God's will for you, which is good and pleasing and perfect. (Rom. 12:1–2, NLT)

The Call to Marriage Reformation

Building on the Rock of Ages is the key to marital endurance and fulfillment. The way forward is going backward to the ancient path in Scripture. Ancient does not mean outdated. The truths of the Ancient of Days transcends time. We can recover the inheritance of our godly ancestors. It is returning to the covenant roots of our Judeo-Christian heritage in marriage and family. It is wholeheartedly returning to the biblical manual on marriage (Matt. 22:37). We must contend for the paradigm of our biblical heritage on marriage. The Spirit will guide us into the truths of the mystery of oneness (Jn. 16:13). The Bible equips husbands and wives to perform every good work for a successful marriage:

> All Scripture is inspired by God and is useful to teach us what is true and to make us realize what is wrong in our lives. It corrects us when we are wrong and teaches us to do what is right. God uses it to prepare and equip his people to do every good work. (2 Tim.3:16–17, NLT)

God is calling this generation to be radical revolutionaries. It is the clarion call to return to the wholeness of Judeo-Christian marriage. It is the call to weary and burdened spouses to come and receive rest in their souls (Matt. 11:28–29). It is entering the strong tower of the Lord where there is security in Him who is faithful and true to guard the marital union "till death do us part" (Ps. 121:7, Mark 10:9). It is a call to the Bride of Christ in this generation, the Church community, to be pioneers for marriage reformation. The generational call is to be pathfinders of the way back home to the ancient foundations of holy matrimony.

I believe Church leadership is rising to advance the cause for marriage reformation in the nuclear family! The *Ekklesia*, the called-out ones, is the seasoning salt of our community. In the ancient Greek democracy, the *Ekklesia* was the ruling governmental council that influenced society with its mandates and principles. The Church is the light of the world. The Church must define marriage to the world, not just in fiat, but in living demonstration of the power of the Spirit.

Statistics for divorce in the Church and the world are almost indistinguishable. But this can change. Our marital statistics must so differ that the world may know we are His disciples (Jn 13:35). When married couples invest in their marriage with the wealth of biblical principles and precepts, blessings are credited to them and future generations. You pass on your values to generations, some of which you will see. But you are also investing in future societies where your labor of love becomes generative blessings.

The book of Hebrews records this principle of investing in future generations. Abraham paid tithes to Melchizedek. The Levites, Abraham's descendants, collected tithes from the people. From God's perspective, the Levites paid tithes to Melchizedek. Abraham's actions were credited to the Levites, for "one might even say that Levi, who collects the tenth, paid the tenth through Abraham" (Heb. 7:9). There are blessings that your ancestors have passed on to you. Pass on a rich marital legacy to future generations. They will rise up and call you blessed!

Serving God's Purpose in Your Generation

Restoring the Judeo-Christian culture to the family can be a challenge for some Christian couples. We do not need to reinvent the wheel. God has an excellent design for marriage and the family in His Word. Contemporary societal norms can be a pervasive force. Rebuilding the ancient marital structures that have been devastated for generations takes courage and tenacious resolve. It is a total transformation of marital direction and expression for some couples.

Christian couples live in the world but should not conform to the world's value system. Jesus prayed for his disciples that the Father would not take them out of the world but protect them from the evil one (Jn. 17:15). He also prayed for all believers down through the ages until "today" (Jn. 17:20–23). Noah lived in an era when there was great wickedness on the earth. But it is recorded that, "In his generation, Noah was a man righteous and wholehearted; Noah walked with God" (Gen. 6:9, CJB). Noah turned his heart toward God, who strengthened him to overcome the influence of his generation. You may be at a crossroads. Here is the Word of the Lord:

"This is what the Lord says: 'Stand at the crossroads and look; ask for the ancient paths, ask where the good way is, and walk in it, and you will find rest for your souls'" (Jer. 6:16).

Christian couples can have the victory of Noah, who was righteous and wholehearted in his generation. A couple's priority is devotion to Christ. Jesus told his disciples that they must love God above everyone, including their spouse (Lk. 14:26). Couples must examine their marital attitudes and behaviors in light of the Scripture and replace ungodly beliefs with the sanctifying Word of truth (Jn. 17:17). The power of the Spirit and the Word will cleanse the mind and transform the heart (Prov. 23:7).

A Radical Pioneering Generation Is Arising

It would take a bold, courageous, and defiant generation to disregard a formidable world system and fully return to God's path of biblical marriage, a dynamic paradigm shift. I believe this generation is here. I have seen them in my office where the marital issue is "marriage enrichment." These young people are in their twenties and thirties. These couples from all walks of life and various churches seek to align with the biblical model. They organize marital retreats to share experiences and discuss communication and conflict resolution within a biblical framework. They are rebuilding the old road for future generations. Interestingly, the husbands in these groups were awakened to the "ancient ways" and were willing to make extraordinary sacrifices for God, their wives, and family.

One of these couples came into counseling as a proactive measure. The wife was pregnant; the husband was about to reenter college for further training and buying their first house. They told me they needed counsel because they faced "some major life issues."

I believe a radical, pioneering generation is here to rebuild the ancient foundations for marital reformation with Jesus Christ, the Cornerstone. They arise to serve God's purpose for their age (Acts 13:36). I believe God has aroused the silver head saints to heal the marriage breach in this generation. I believe God has prepared a mature generation with marital experience "attained in the way of righteousness" to mantle the youthful generation (Prov. 16:31). God has raised spiritually aged intercessors stoking the holy fires for marriage renewal. May God raise up more seasoned couples with wisdom, counsel, power, and understanding to contend for this aspiring generation for societal transformation. May the Ancient of Days impart increasing oneness to those who desire to pursue the high calling of marriage in glorifying God (Matt. 5:16).

Bibliography

Armstrong, Patti Maguire. Integrated Catholic Life. *Grace Trumps Dysfunction in Marriage, 2014.*

Chambers, Oswald(Author) and James Reimann(Editor). *My Utmost for His Highest.* Grand Rapids: Our Daily Bread Publishing: 2017.

Cloud, Henry, and John Townsend. *How People Grow: What the Bible Reveals about Personal Growth.* Grand Rapids: Zondervan, 2004.

Campos-Duffy, Rachael. *Stay Home, Stay Happy: 10 Secrets to Loving At-home Motherhood.* New York: New American Library, 2009.

Canfield, Ken. *The Heart of Father: How You Can Become a Dad of Destiny.* Chicago: North Field Publishing, 2006.

Evans, Anthony T., and Crystal Evans Hurst. *Kingdom Woman.* Illinois: Tyndale House Publishers, 2013.

Evans, Anthony T. *Kingdom Man.* Illinois: Tyndale House Publishers, 2012.

Garr, John D. Family Sanctuary: Restoring the Biblically Hebraic Home. Atlanta: Golden Key Press, 2003.

Garr, John D. *Bless You! Restoring the Power of Biblical Blessings.* Atlanta: Restoration Foundation, 2005.

Garr, John D. *Family Worship: Making Your Home a House of God.* Atlanta: Golden Key Press, 2013.

MacArthur, John. *Stand Firm: Living in a Post-Christian Culture.* Sanford: Ligonier Ministries, 2020.

Olson, David, and Karen Olson. *Prepare Enrich.* www.pre-pare-enrich.com

Sheets, Dutch. *The Pleasure of His Company: A Journey to Intimate Friendship with God.* Minneapolis: Bethany House Publishers, 2014.

Stanton, Glen T. Focus on the Family. *What Research says about Couples who Pray Together, 2019.*

Strong, James. Strong's Exhaustive Concordance of the Bible. Carol Stream: Tyndale House Publishers, 2009.

The Barna Group. *New Marriage and Divorce Statistics Released: Family and Kids,* 2008.

Wilbur, Paul. *Touching the Heart of God: Embracing the Calendar of the Kingdom.* Apopka: Certa Books, 2015.

Wilson, Hobson I. "The Effects of Web-based Parenting Education on Father Involvement." D.Min. diss., Southern Christian University, 2003.

About the Author

Dr. Irving Wilson is a pastoral counselor and marriage and family life educator. He previously served as a guidance counselor in Florida Public Schools. Irving has ministered as a Christian counselor for over 18 years on the staff of three Christian counseling organizations.

Dr. Wilson obtained a Bachelor's degree in Education from the University of the Southern Caribbean and a Master's degree in Counselor Education from Florida Atlantic University. He holds a Doctor of Ministry degree in Family Therapy from Amridge University. He is a Board Certified Christian Counselor with the Board of Christian Professional and Pastoral Counseling and a marriage facilitator with Prepare/Enrich.

Irving and his wife, Sherron, are originally from the Caribbean Island of Grenada and now live in Ft. Lauderdale, Florida. They have been married for over 27 years. They have three adult sons: Nigel, Alexander, and David.